# POUND THE STONE

# POUND THE STONE

## 7 LESSONS TO DEVELOP GRIT ON THE PATH TO MASTERY

Joshua Medcalf

ISBN-13: 9780692887622
ISBN-10: 0692887628

# CONTENTS

# DON'T READ THIS....

I'm so excited for you to read this story, and I hope that it encourages and inspires you on this journey we call life. Before you start though, while this book is a stand alone fable from a story perspective, the principles and wisdom build upon what I shared in *Chop Wood Carry Water*. This book is very much the 201 version. **Many of those foundational principles and the wisdom from Chop Wood are not in here, so we highly suggest you read *Chop Wood Carry Water* before starting this book, especially if you are using it with your team.**

While this story is a fable, most of the stories within are based on true stories from my life and the lives of my friends, clients, and acquaintances.

We are grateful to be apart of your journey!

(*I like you, you little rebel!*)

Love,

Joshua Michael Medcalf

# BEFORE YOU START....

Make sure you go to *poundthestone.com* to download the free **Pound The Stone Motivational Mixtape,** as well as stickers and other gear that are available for purchase.

We have also created a**, Pound The Stone Training Manual**, that is great for group discussions and personal introspection. It is available on Amazon.

As you read, and after you finish, please share your favorite chapters, quotes, and excerpts on social media and tag me!

Twitter: @joshuamedcalf

Instagram: @realjoshuamedcalf

# CHAPTER 1

## ENOUGH IS ENOUGH

"You're done."

The words drove through Jason's chest like an ice pick, and he felt the familiar rush of angry blood. WHAM!! Without thinking, he slammed his hand onto the desk in front of him.

"That's not fair! State finals are in two days!" he yelled.

Across from him, Coach Michael's tired face didn't waver. This was the face of a man who'd had enough. "Doesn't matter. I can't have you on this team anymore, Jason. You punched an opposing player in the face. You almost lost us the game."

"You saw it, he was giving me cheap shots all game. Trey always does that! He had it coming!"

"I don't want excuses. I just want your gear turned in by 8 a.m. tomorrow."

Jason reeled, desperate. He knew he pushed the boundaries a lot, but he never thought it would go this far. His fists balled in rage, clenching and unclenching.

"So this is how it goes, huh?" He glared at his Coach. "After all your talk about 'team is family'?! I should have known you would quit on me, just like everyone else!"

Michael snapped back at him angrily, "Jason, it's only your freshmen year and you've already failed a drug test, been suspended twice, and accused of cheating on tests several times. I've done my best to make this work for both of us, but I'm not a magician. There are some mistakes I can't cover you on. Enough is enough. You are off this basketball team, son."

Jason blinked, stunned. Those were words he'd never expected to hear. From the time he could walk, basketball was life. With a father in and out of prison, and with a single mother who worked two jobs, the game had become his anchor. He was good at it, too. It felt as natural as breathing. To Jason, a life without basketball was a life without breathing.

Emotion choked him, but he shoved it down. If there was one thing he'd learned growing up on the streets, it was that men don't cry: they <u>fight</u>. He knew he had one last shot at changing Michael's mind, so he had to appeal to what he cared about more than anything else: winning. "Coach, I scored 28 points in the semis. You know you can't win State without me!"

Coach's eyes flashed. Winning really may have been the thing he cared about most, and Jason was easily one of his best players. He had the kind of raw natural talent that could shift a game on a dime, and it had led them to several clutch wins already that season. But after a second, that hungry look in Michael's eyes faded. It was replaced with resolution instead.

"You know what? You're probably right. You have incredible natural talent, Jason. But you're too big of a liability. I've made some poor choices to indulge your complete lack of character in the past, but those stop now. I don't even want you sitting on the bench at State. Besides the state board would most likely suspend you for three games anyway, so this is on you, not me. *Your choice has created your challenge.* You've lost the privilege to be a part of this team."

Jason blinked, and a roar like a stereo blast turned up in his ears. His jaw clenched tight, his chest heaved as he stood up, drawing all six-foot-four of himself to his full height. With his bright bleached Mohawk, he stood even taller. Most people got intimidated by his physical presence, but not Coach. He was still talking. Still, Jason was too angry to listen. He felt the rage building inside him, and as he turned to leave, it happened: without thinking, Jason drew back--

WHAM!! He punched his clenched fist straight through the drywall of the office. The drywall powdered and caved in easily enough, but the thick wood behind it didn't.

They both heard the sound at the same time: a loud hollow POP! like a piece of wood snapping. As the lightning bolt of pain slashed up Jason's forearm, he knew that he'd just broken a lot more than some drywall.

# CHAPTER 2

# LAST CHANCE

"I can't believe I'm saying this. But you have one last chance."

Pacing in front of Jason was Scott Miles, Athletic Director for the Midvale High Raiders. He stopped and looked Jason in the eye. "To be honest, you don't deserve it. But thanks to your coach and your team captain, you're getting it."

A week had passed since Jason put his fist through that office wall. The cast covering his hand itched, frustrating him. At first he faced expulsion, but after Coach Michael had calmed down, a solution was presented. It wasn't perfect, but it was better than being off the team for good.

So Jason did his best to play along, "So, I'm doing this all summer?"

Coach nodded, handing Jason a flyer. "Yes. The program is twelve weeks. You'll start with a week of sales training, then you'll hit the streets."

"All I have to do is sell books door to door, and I get to keep a percentage of the sales?"

"If it sounds easy, let me tell you right now: it's not. This isn't exactly summer camp. Many of the students who sign up, never finish. If you're one of them, that's that; you'll never play ball in this district again."

"But if I finish, I'm back on the team?"

"Finish? You're going to need to do a lot more than finish. You have to hit the numbers."

Jason just grinned. "C'mon, Coach. I'll hit the numbers. How many do I need to sell?"

"Two hundred."

"Easy enough." Jason was feeling good.

Michael chuckled, "Not two hundred total, son. Two hundred <u>per book</u>."

"Oh... how many books are there?"

"Take a look."

Jason scanned the list of books on the sheet --

*The Slight Edge*
*Chop Wood Carry Water*
*Grit*
*The Only Way to Win*
*Daring Greatly*
*In a Pit with a Lion on a Snowy Day*

<u>Six</u>. Jason's smile fell as he did the quick math. 1,200 books. That was a LOT of books.

A.D. Miles noticed and chuckled. "Like he said, Jason: this will be the toughest summer of your life. Twelve to fourteen hours a day of pounding the streets. You still want to sign up?"

Jason nodded, resolved. "If it means I can play ball again, then I'm in."

Miles shrugged. "Alright, then. Do you have the release?"

Jason handed over the form, which his mother had signed after discussing it with Coach. The program meant Jason would be staying in a stranger's home all summer, covering a territory at least two hours from home. But after the past year of dealing with her son's disciplinary issues, his mother didn't think twice. "When I was 14, I had to drop out of school to work ten hours a day in a cannery. Don't tell me you think selling books is harder, young man. You love to talk your way out of everything, so let's see you use that smile and smooth tongue for something worthwhile."

Jason was angry, but he knew by now not to expect his life to be fair. Everyone seemed to have it better and easier than he did. But this was his only path back to basketball, so if he had to do something this stupid to get there, fine. He stuffed everything into his backpack and shook Coach's hand, putting on a brave face, "Thanks, Coach. I'll see you in the fall."

"Remember Jason, this is your last chance. Don't come back if you haven't hit your numbers."

"Did they go for it?" Jason nodded, fist-bumping his teammate Travis, who'd been sitting out in the hall waiting.

Travis was two years older than him, and though his background couldn't have been more different from Jason's, he always went out of his way to make sure Jason was taken care of. Jason had always heard that teams need "glue," but that never made sense until he met Travis. Even though he was one of those guys who just seemed to have it all – Class President, lettered in every sport, a consistent top rank in his class

6

academically – he seemed to always put his teammates first. In fact, it was his suggestion that even got Coach thinking about giving Jason another shot in the first place.

"Thank you so much! I owe you for life, man," Jason tried to sound as grateful as he felt.

But Travis shrugged it off, "No worries buddy. We need you on the court next year, so I had to make it happen! Who knows, maybe you'll make some good money while you're at it!"

# CHAPTER 3

## KAIYA

Jason laid on the bus bench looking up at the sky, rap music blasting through his headphones. It was the only way he could tune out his anger. He knew punching the wall was a big mistake, but he felt like Coach was going extra hard on him. Coach loved winning more than anything, and Jason's fight had cost them the championship. Without Jason, they lost by 25 points in the finals.

He sat up, trying to block it all out. That's when he saw her. The girl down the bench from him seemed familiar, like they'd been in a class together. He thought he'd seen her before. But not like this.

She was clearly a beautiful girl, some kind of mix of Asian and possibly Jamaican, but it wasn't just that she was exotic, there was something different in the way she carried herself. Not like other girls. She sat up straight, her foot bouncing as it crossed her long, shapely leg. He noticed she wore heels and a blazer, like she worked in an office. *Who did that in high school?*

He caught her eye and smiled, pulling his headphones off. "Hi. I like your shoes."

She popped an earbud out, looking more than a bit annoyed. "What?"

"I like your shoes. You going somewhere fancy?"

"Kind of. They're for a job interview."

"Where? Not at McDonald's, huh?"

He laughed at his own joke, but she didn't blink. "I already did that for two years. I'm upgrading. It's a real estate company downtown. They need a receptionist."

"Aren't you too young for an office job like that?"

Her eyes flashed with a look of defiance. "Only if they know how old I am, and I only have to tell them if they ask. I'll never know if I don't try, right?"

"Yeah, I guess." Jason trailed off, looking at the book she held. "What're you reading? It doesn't look like a textbook."

"It's not. It's called *Hustle*. It's the story of a guy who went from living in the closet of a gym and serving in a homeless shelter to building a million-dollar brand. He shares his journey and all the lessons he learned along the way."

"Is that why you're reading it? You wanna be a CEO or something some day?"

Kaiya answered with quiet confidence, "I don't just want to. I already am."

Jason was surprised: he wasn't used to seeing that kind of confidence from girls. Honestly, he wasn't used to seeing that kind of confidence from anyone. "So, you're a CEO?" She nodded. Jason continued, "Of what?"

"*InspireU*, my tutoring business. I have four clients already. I tutor kids in writing, reading comprehension, and study habits. I'll start doing AP Lit and English next year."

"For real?" She nodded with the swagger of a pro athlete. Jason shifted, "Wait a minute. So if you already have a business, why are you going to this real estate place to ask for another job?"

"Once the business grows, I'll need an office. I don't know anything about real estate, but if I work there I can learn."

Jason nodded, impressed. She really wasn't like any girl he'd ever met before. "So when you get your office, what name is going on the door?"

She smiled, held out her hand. "Kaiya."

Jason smiled back, shaking. "Jason."

"I know." Before Jason could ask her how she knew, she got up. "My car is here." Sure enough, a black Honda Accord pulled to a stop at the curb.

As she stood to leave, Jason realized, "Wait! I didn't get your number!"

She smirked, "Bye Jason," and got in the car.

It drove off, leaving Jason's mind blown. *"Kaiya."* He repeated it. He wouldn't forget the name.

# CHAPTER 4

# POUND THE STONE

THE ENERGY IN the hotel conference room was powerful, but Jason had never felt more out of place. He sat surrounded by hundreds of other student sales trainees, none of whom looked anything like him. No athletes, certainly, mostly honor roll types.

Thankfully the lights went down, and the program director took the mic. "We have a real treat for y'all tonight, and I'm so excited we're able to bring this guy in as our keynote speaker. He is a five-time world champion, two-time MVP, three-time Finals MVP, and Rookie of the Year. He is also a 15-time All-Star, and... well, you all know who he is. To me, he's just one of the kindest, hardest-working, and most down to earth people I've ever known: T.D.!"

Jason's jaw dropped as the room applauded, standing at attention.

The man taking the stage seemed to fill the whole room with his presence, but there was a quiet strength in every movement. It was the same quiet strength that Jason had idolized growing up, watching this man win championship after championship on TV. But here in this room, with no screen in between them, he seemed both larger than he realized, but also more human. He nodded humbly to the program director before taking the mic.

"Thank you all." The applause faded, and T.D. paced. "I want to talk to all of you today about mastery. About becoming the best in the world at something. You see, there's a secret that you may not have heard about how to get there. It's something that only the very best in the world know how to do, and it's the little thing they do that sets them so far apart from everyone else. In fact, I believe it is the only thing *anyone* can do to gain true mastery at anything, and it's an equal opportunity principle. It can be applied to fulfill your potential in business, in sports, in your relationships, as well as your overall life. Do you want to know what it is?"

Jason leaned forward, eager. Now this was something he wanted to hear!

Sensing the excitement in the room, T.D. grinned. "Okay, here it is. The one thing that the very best know how to do that so many others don't, the same thing they've all used to get where they are, is this: they know how to pound the stone. But knowing isn't enough. Pounding the stone has become a lifestyle for them."

Jason was puzzled, curious. He'd never heard the phrase before. On stage, the big man went on, "This philosophy comes from a poem that I know very well, because it hangs on the wall in my team's locker room. I probably know it better than any other set of words in the English language..."

T.D. paused, eyes closed, reciting it from somewhere deep inside of himself: "*When nothing seems to help, I go and look at a stonecutter hammering away at his rock perhaps a hundred times without as much as a crack showing in it. Yet at the hundred and first blow it will split in two, and I know it was not that blow that did it, but all that had gone before.*"

He opened his eyes again, scanning the room. "Now, I've never met a single person who just wanted to be average. On the other hand, I've met thousands of people who want to be great. But here's the thing I've learned about *wanting* to be great: everyone wants to be great, until it's time to do what greatness requires.

The hard truth is this: *greatness requires more grit, determination, character, and persistence than nearly any member of the human race are willing to develop.* How many Michael Phelps are there? How many Steve Jobs? How many Oprahs? How many Steph Currys?

I would guess that there are a lot of talented people in this room. Unfortunately, talent is overrated. But the ability to pound the stone, day in and day out, year after year, until finally the stone splits? *That is the rarest, most valuable asset on the planet.* And I guarantee that if you can develop it, you <u>will</u> become great in whatever you do.

Now, the program you're about to go into gives you an incredible opportunity to put this philosophy to work and cut your teeth in the street. It's designed to push you to the brink of yourselves and help you develop the kind of character and grit that is almost impossible to develop in other places, but I can promise you that you'll only get out of it what you put into it.

So, will you pound the stone this summer? Will you lean in every time you experience setbacks and failures? Will you continue to pound the stone no matter how many doors slam in your face, no matter how many "No's" you hear, no matter how tempting it is to quit?

When you face the choice between doing the hard thing or taking the easy way out... will you pound the stone?

When you face the choice to tackle a challenge or run from it... will you pound the stone?

When you face the choice to treat a person poorly or well in a tough situation... will you pound the stone?

When you face the choice to keep showing up or to quit.... will you pound the stone?

I certainly hope that in all of these situations, you'll choose to pound the stone. But at the end of the day, no one can choose but you. And for some of you, that's scary. You'll be on your own this summer. No one will tell you what to do, what time to start, or what time to finish. So the temptation will be to not pound the stone for twelve to fourteen hours a day, because no one is making you. But if you can push past that, and pound the stone and give your very best day in and day out, you will be amazed at *who you become through this process.*

Remember, everyone wants to be great, until it's time to do what greatness requires. I can tell you from experience, that it requires you to faithfully and persistently pound the stone regardless of your temporary feelings."

T.D. put his hands together like a monk and gave a slight bow as the place erupted in a standing ovation and thunderous applause.

## CHAPTER 5

# THE SMALLEST HOUSE ON THE BLOCK

JASON SHRUGGED HIS backpack off, wiping sweat from his face. His t-shirt stuck to his back, and his wrist felt like fire ants had crawled inside to sting every inch of his skin. It was a hundred degrees already, and it wasn't even noon.

On Monday, flying high with motivation fresh off of T.D.'s speech, Jason had been stoked. But by today – Friday – he was ready to give up. He hated this stupid job.

After the week of training, he and the other students had been sent to their different territories, where they stayed in a hotel while they knocked on doors to find someone who was willing to host them for the summer. The sales program even provided a list of pre-approved households that had either hosted student salespeople before, or were connected to the program in some other way.

But even with that head start, Jason still hadn't found a host. He couldn't believe that it wasn't the honor roll kids, but him – the big athletic guy with the charming smile who could always talk his way out of trouble – *he* was the one who was striking out.

Yesterday he got so discouraged he just gave up at lunch and went back to the hotel. But a single thought kept dogging him: if he didn't do this, he had zero chance of playing basketball again.

So that morning he hit the streets again, going down the list of the last few houses. The first three had been "no's," and one woman had even slammed the door in his face.

Only one house remained, and Jason wanted nothing to do with it. It was the smallest house on the block, and instead of a new Tahoe or Tesla in the driveway like the other houses, this one had the ugliest car Jason had ever seen. It was a boxy old Subaru in a weird color that bothered him. "What kind of person drives a car like that?" He thought to himself.

But Jason didn't have a choice. It was this house, or the end of his basketball dream. He took a deep breath and knocked.

"Hello?" The door cracked open, revealing a slender, 60-year-old woman whose crystal blue eyes shone intensely like spotlights. He got the sense that this lady didn't mess around.

"Hi, I'm Jason." He tried to smile convincingly as he explained who he was. Once he mentioned the name of his program, the woman's face lit up as she swung the door open.

"Oh, come on in! Do you want some lemonade? My name is Jan, by the way."

Inside, the house was nice and neat, everything cleaned and polished and in its place. There was no clutter. Somehow it seemed bigger and nicer on the inside than it looked from the street.

"Russ, come meet this bright young man from the book sales program!" Jan called, as she poured Jason an ice-cold lemonade in the kitchen.

A moment later, her husband entered. He was almost as tall as Jason with a broad, lined face, and a set of shoulders that looked like he might have been a pro football player in his younger years. He offered his hand and smiled warmly. "Nice to meet you, I'm Russ."

His grip was like iron. And it made sense. He wore the uniform of a manual laborer: a pair of utility pants, and a stained work shirt with a patch that said, *City Sanitation Services.* Jason thought they seemed a bit of an odd couple for this upper middle class neighborhood.

As they sat at the kitchen table, Jason asked if he might stay with them for the summer. Russ didn't even blink. "Of course!"

Jan chimed in, "We only ask that you pull your weight and clean up after yourself. Dinner is at seven every night. I appreciate punctuality."

Jason just smiled, "Yeah."

Russ's voice dropped an octave, stern. "Excuse me? In this house you will be treated with respect, and you will treat us with the same respect. It's 'yes ma'am,' and 'yes sir.' Is that clear?"

"Yes, sir." Jason replied, slightly embarrassed.

"Glad that is settled," Jan replied warmly. "Now, we can put you in the guest bedroom, just follow me…"

As she showed him around, Jason breathed a sigh of relief. He was grateful to be here, even if this place wasn't the best-looking house on the block. Even though Russ had corrected him, there was something warm and good about him and Jan. Somehow, he knew they cared deeply about him. It wasn't something Jason had felt much in his life.

That night, as he lay in the small guest room that would be his bedroom for the rest of the summer, he was excited. Now, finally, he could get down to business.

# CHAPTER 6

# DO IT ANYWAY

THE NEXT MORNING, Jason woke up to the smell of fresh coffee. Russ was in the kitchen, eating the steaming-hot breakfast that Jan had just made. As Jason joined him, he looked him in the eye and asked, "So, are you ready for your first day?"

Through a mouthful of bacon, Jason admitted, "Not really. I've never done a job like this before, so I don't really know what I'm doing. And I don't know if my training was enough."

"Good."

"What's that supposed to mean?!" Jason huffed with attitude.

"Well, one thing I've learned on my journey is that you are never truly ready. *The only way you get prepared and ready is by actually experiencing the thing you are afraid of doing, but that you know in your gut you are supposed to do. The timing will never be right. There is no such thing as perfect timing.* Let me ask you a question: what would happen if you turned your 'What if's' into 'Even if's'?"

"What do you mean?"

"I mean that instead of asking yourself...

*What if this fails?*
*What if no one purchases it?*
*What if I'm not good enough?*

You started telling yourself these instead...

*Even if this fails...*
*Even if no one purchases it...*
*Even if I'm not good enough... (yet)*

Start to see your life as a story Jason, and remember that every great story has plot twists, trials and hardships. We love stories where the unlikely hero overcomes adversity and chooses to act in spite of facing seemingly impossible odds. What is the worst thing that can happen if you sell zero books this summer but approach it with a growth mindset? You still gain invaluable experience; you still learn and grow. What if you approach this summer like Conor McGregor approaches every fight? According to him, *'I never lose: either I win or I learn.'*"

Jason was surprised by how confidently Russ was speaking about something so deep, so he just nodded along, letting him continue.

"Jason, something corrodes and dies inside of you when you refuse to pursue what sets your soul on fire in order to play it safe. You weren't created to play it safe. The greatest risk of all is playing it safe, and I refuse to believe the purpose of life is to arrive safely at death. The unlikely hero of your story is <u>you</u>, and if you play it safe, you may not like how your story turns out.

The fear will always be there. *Do it anyway.*

19

The lack of resources is real. *Do it anyway.*

The lack of experience might set you back. *Do it anyway.*

YOU are the unlikely hero. *Do it anyway.*

I think Macklemore summed it up really well in his song *10,000 Hours*: 'The greats weren't great because at birth they could paint, the greats were great because they paint a lot.' There will always be obstacles, set-backs, and legitimate excuses not to do what you know in your gut you should do. <u>Do it anyway</u>."

Jason just nodded politely, "Thanks, Russ. I appreciate the advice. I guess now I'm going to go out and 'do it anyway'!"

But as he walked out the door, Jason couldn't help but chuckle. This guy probably picked up trash and swept streets for a living. What in the world was he talking about? He sure said some strange things. Jason wondered if Russ secretly struggled with delusions of grandeur.

# CHAPTER 7

## DEFINING SUCCESS

JASON KNEW THIS job wasn't going to be easy, so he wasn't surprised when the first few doors he knocked on didn't lead to sales. But just before lunch, he stopped at a children's learning center. After his pitch, he was expecting the usual "Sorry, we're not interested."

But instead, the woman just smiled as she looked the books over. "We'll take five of each."

Jason couldn't believe it. After getting the paperwork signed, he walked down the street with a huge smile. He just sold thirty books! That energy must have been contagious, because later that afternoon he sold twenty-five more to a community library. He felt so good about it that he even punched out early. Fifty-five books was a solid day's work, and at this rate, he'd be able to hit his target of 1,200 books early.

Dinner that night was a big delicious spread of home cooking that made Jason's mouth water. After Russ said grace, he dug in.

As he did, Jan looked up from her plate, "So, Jason. What are you grateful for today?"

Jason grinned. "Well, I made my first two sales today. Fifty-five books."

Russ nodded, "That must have felt good."

"It did! So I guess you could say I'm grateful that my first day was a success."

Jan glanced at Russ, who smiled. "Success. That's an interesting little word."

"How so?"

"Well, it means very different things, depending on who you ask... I guess it depends on how you define '*success*.' How do you define success Jason?" Russ's eyes were glued to Jason.

"Umm, I don't know..." Jason realized he hadn't thought about this much. "I guess I would say achieving your goals, making enough money to do what you want, and not having to struggle."

By the disappointed look on Russ's face, Jason wondered if he had some-how said something wrong. Before he could ask, Jan jumped in, empa-thetic. "That is definitely one way to define it. Let me tell you a story about a guy named Dave that might help you understand the impor-tance of defining success well. You see, Dave was a musician, and when he was a few years older than you, his band was about to record their first major album. They'd been flown to New York City and were just days away from recording, when the other band members decided they no longer wanted Dave in the band."

Jason's head shot up, "Man, if that happened to me, I'd be furious!"

"I can only imagine what you would have done." Jan chuckled, glanc-ing at his cast. "So, on his bus ride back to Los Angeles, Dave decided that he was going to start a new band, and he determined what success would look like for this band and his life. Success would be making more money, getting more girls, selling more albums, and becoming more famous than those other guys. He decided to recycle his pain and use it to fuel his training and mastery."

Jason nodded, curious. "So what happened?!"

"Over the next ten years his band started to sell a lot of albums, eventually eclipsing more than 15 million in sales as they toured across the world. And many people consider Dave Mustaine and his band *Megadeth* to be one of the pioneer legends of hard rock and roll."

Jason's eyes went wide. "Wow! I mean, hard rock's not really my style, but I know those guys. That's a really cool story!"

"Oh, but the story doesn't end there. Remember, this is about the importance of how you define success. A few years ago, Dave broke down in tears in an interview and admitted that he still sees himself as a failure."

Jason couldn't believe it. "What? How in the world could he believe that?"

"Because the band he got kicked out of was Metallica." Jan replied.

Jason's mouth dropped open in shock, as she continued. "Because Dave had defined success as being bigger and better than Metallica, he was never able to see his band as successful, no matter how many albums they sold or tours they booked. It's a dangerous lesson. If you aren't careful, Jason, you can end up defining success using metrics that aren't really valuable, and ending up with a version of 'success' that – like Dave – actually feels more like failure.

Instead, it might be more helpful to think about it this way: how will you define success on your deathbed? Typically, people say the three things that really mattered were who they became as a person, the impact they had on others, and whether they lived the life they knew they were supposed to live. Russ and I can't tell you how to define success for yourself, but it is something you should definitely think about."

Russ cleared his throat, "One of my favorite quotes is from a guy named Francis Chan, who said, '*Our greatest fear in life should not be of failure, but of succeeding at things in life that don't really matter.*'

**Every day, people head out the door believing that everything will be different if they can just achieve more, win more, or make more money. But if achievement hasn't filled that void yet, how is achieving more going to fill it in the future? Like thirsty people guzzling salt water, achievement only creates a greater desire for accomplishing more, dehydrating us of true satisfaction and fulfillment.**

One of my greatest fears has always been getting to the end of my life and the top of the ladder, and realizing that my ladder has been on the wrong building all along. You want to make sure your ladder is on the right building, Jason."

Jason nodded, lost in thought. As he finished dinner, he stood up to walk back to the guest room.

"Excuse me?" Jan smiled as she looked at Jason. He paused, confused. "Pull your weight, remember? You can clear the table and dry the dishes, since you have a cast."

"Oh, I'm sorry. I was still thinking about that story and I completely forgot." he nodded, and went to work.

As he crawled into bed that night, Jason thought it over. The story Jan had told was powerful, but he couldn't help but wonder if that was how she and Russ rationalized their place in the world. They drove the worst car on the block and had the smallest house. The people Jason looked up to drove cool cars, got lots of hot girls, and made tons of money. Jason was grateful for Russ and Jan's help, but when push came to shove he was going to trust the definition of success that actually came from someone successful, not from this couple.

# CHAPTER 8

# CUT THE ROPES

ONE NIGHT, AS Jason was returning from the day's work and a gleaming blacked-out Porsche 911 zoomed past him, pulling into the driveway a few doors down. The driver was in his 30's, and looked like Brad Pitt – tan, blonde haired, wearing a custom-fitting three-piece suit that looked like a million bucks. He waved at Russ as he went inside, and Jason shook his head in awe.

"Who is that?" he asked Russ.

"Our neighbor Andrew, he's a great guy."

"What does he do for a living?"

"He's an investment banker, at one of the big firms downtown." Russ noticed Jason's face fall a little bit as he sighed. "What's wrong? You look like I just told you Santa Claus isn't real."

"It's nothing, just... I know that guys like me don't get jobs like that."

"Are you sure about that?"

"Yeah, pretty sure."

Russ got an intense look in his eyes. "Sounds like you have a rope to cut."

"What? What does rope have to do with being a stockbroker?"

"Everything! A man once took his children to the zoo in India while on vacation. Their last stop was the zoo's prized animals: the elephants. These massive beasts roamed around freely, with nothing but a single rope tied to a stick carried by one of the zookeepers to hold them back.

The man's face went white and he grabbed his kids and backed away. He shouted at the zookeeper, 'Are you insane?! You have two-ton beasts just roaming around here tied down only by a single rope?! They could snap that at any time and crush everything in their path!'

The zookeeper just smiled, 'Sir! Please calm down. I know how powerful they are. But what you don't know is that when they are born, the very first thing we do is tie a rope around their leg. We tie the other end of the rope around a strong tree. When they are young, the rope is much stronger than them. They fight and fight and fight to break free from the rope, but eventually their will breaks, and they come to believe that they can never break free from the rope. As they grow older, they do so with the belief that the rope has power over them. Even though they have massive potential and are amazingly powerful, they will never hurt us. Their belief about the rope holds them back.'"

Jason nodded, "I think I see what you're getting at."

"I hope so, Jason. The question you always have to ask yourself is, 'What are the ropes in my life that have been holding me back? What beliefs am I clinging to that are keeping me stuck? A wise friend of mine once told me, *we learn our belief systems as very little children and then move through life creating experiences to match our beliefs.*"[1]

---

1 Louise Hay

Jason took a deep breath as he was deeply moved by this idea.

"Jason, most people are completely unaware of this. They just float down-stream through life. You must always ask yourself, what are the beliefs that may have been true at one point in my life, but are no longer true and are keeping me from fulfilling my greatest potential? Maybe it's something as simple as thinking that guys like you can't become stock-brokers like Andrew. But you'd be very wrong there. Do you know who Chris Gardner is?"

"His name sounds familiar..."

"And it should. He's the man whose journey as a homeless single dad was made into the film, *Pursuit of Happyness.* He worked his way out of total poverty to become an incredibly successful stockbroker, and had a long and very prosperous career."

Jason nodded, "Wow, I didn't know that."

"Jason, it's easy to look around the world and say things like, 'guys like me don't get jobs like that,' but it's just not true. Whenever you find your-self thinking that, ask yourself: 'Who says?'

You aren't smart enough. 'Who says?'
You need another degree to be successful in this economy. 'Who says?'
You are too old. 'Who says?'
You are too young. 'Who says?'
You don't have enough experience. 'Who says?'
You can never play for that team or in that league. 'Who says?'

These false beliefs are all around us, and many times we don't even know what they are until they are broken. So, we must continually ask, 'Who says?' And we must continually re-examine our beliefs to see if they are true, or if they're just a rope that needs to be cut."

The more Jason thought about his own beliefs about himself and the world, the more it made sense. "Yeah, I think I might have a few of those."

"Well, now you know what to do with them," Russ smiled. "Cut the ropes!"

# CHAPTER 9

# PAPER CEILINGS

THE NEXT DAY, the sales didn't come easily. By the time Jason's stomach growled for dinner, he had only sold two books. He walked home frustrated, but he knew what would help clear his head: basketball. He had passed some courts at a park a few blocks from Russ and Jan's house, so after dinner and helping with the dishes, that's exactly where he went.

He planned on hitting his sales goal and making the team again. And when he did, he needed to be ready. Even though he had always hated it, he needed to practice. Games were his time to shine, and he knew that he always played much better in front of a crowd. He fed off that energy and attention. Practice, on the other hand, felt more like torture.

So when he saw a pickup game starting, he asked if he could join. The guy in charge, Smokey, looked Jason over. "You sure you can play with one hand like that?"

One of the other guys just laughed. "Smokey, c'mon man. Kid has a cast on. Won't be fair."

Jason's competitive side kicked in, and he glared back, "Won't be fair for me, or for you?" That was it; they couldn't let Jason show them up like that. Jason was in, and the game was <u>on</u>.

Street ball was how Jason learned basketball in grade school. But after years of playing in school leagues he forgot how rough and fast it was.

Elbows, traveling, cheap shots. Anything goes on the street and Jason wasn't ready for it. He had gotten soft. He lost the ball twice in the first five possessions, and it quickly became clear that in spite of his natural athleticism, he was simply getting out-played. Without both hands, his dribbling and passing were off. The only thing that saved him was his solid footwork, but even that could only go so far.

By the time the game ended, he had scored just a single layup. He left the court in a burst of hot anger and shame, walking away and trying to ignore the digs the other guys got in at him.

His frustration must have been pretty obvious, because as he got home, Russ looked up from the book he was reading on the porch and asked, "What's wrong?"

Jason just shook his head, "Nothing."

"You look like you're ready to put a cast on the other hand. That's not nothing."

Jason hesitated, then sat down. "Playing with one hand is so frustrating. I'm losing to guys I'm way better than. But with this stupid cast on, it just feels impossible!"

Russ shrugged. "Well, who was responsible for breaking your hand in the first place?"

"What?" Jason was stunned. But he knew Russ was right.

"Jason, I want to tell you a story about '*impossible.*' A little five-year-old boy named Garrett[2] was once diagnosed with a brain tumor. The surgery to remove it saved his life, but left him temporarily paralyzed, deaf, and

---

2  Story comes from the book, *The Art of Work*, by Jeff Goins

31

blind. He would have to learn every motor function over again. About six months later, his dad took him to see a blind athlete who competed in triathlons. Garrett was so inspired, he asked his mom to help him ride his bike when they got back home.

Garrett had barely regained enough of his sight to see blurry objects, and he was able to walk, but very slowly. His mom reluctantly agreed. One year after surgery, Garrett was competing in his first triathlon on a tandem bicycle with his father. By the time he was eighteen years old he had completed a half Ironman, a triathlon, climbed Machu Picchu, and become an Eagle Scout."

Jason, always remember that *when someone tells you something is 'impossible,' what that really means is that it would take more sacrifice, grit, discipline, failure, and persistence than they are willing to give.* One of my favorite guys who won an NBA championship said his dad always told him, *'life is about breaking through paper ceilings.'*[3]

Once you cut the ropes that keep you tied down, then you can start breaking through the paper ceilings above you. Life is full of paper ceilings. Things that are commonplace today were thought impossible a generation ago. A hundred years ago, the idea that a human being could run a mile in under four minutes seemed impossible. But in 1954, a British medical student named Roger Bannister ran a mile in three minutes, fifty-nine point four seconds. Just forty-six days later, an Australian runner named John Landy beat his time. And within three years, over twenty athletes around the world had done the same. Why is that? Did the human race suddenly all get faster? No. They just realized the truth: *that the four-minute mark was a paper ceiling.*

---

3  Kenny Smith

Don't ever let a paper ceiling stop you, Jason. Things that might seem impossible for most people will remain that way because they let a paper ceiling stop them. But for someone with tenacious grit, 'impossible' really is only a word. Our world has perpetually been driven forward by those people, the ones who have believed the impossible was possible with grit, trust, and patience, and who were willing to take responsibility for what they have control over."

# CHAPTER 10

## INCHES AND NAILS

JASON STILL FOUND it hard to practice. After a long day knocking on doors, the last thing he felt like doing was going to the court to run footwork drills and finishing moves around the basket. When Russ asked him about it, he shrugged it off. "It's hard getting used to a different setup. At school we have a whole gym and everything. Here I just have a ball and the courts at the park."

"Isn't that all you had growing up?"

Jason felt himself flush with embarrassment. "Well, yeah, but I don't really have any drills either, I'm used to running them with the team and having Coach telling us what to do. Now I just kind of try to shoot around, but I don't know how much good that's going to do."

Russ nodded, looking at Jason for a long time. Then, "I think I know someone who might be able to help you."

The next day, Russ wasn't home at dinner. But Jan gave Jason a note with an address and a time on it: "8:30pm, tomorrow." When Jason asked what it was about, Jan only shrugged. "He just said you need to be there on time and ready to work out." Jason wondered what this meant. Russ was a street sweeper. Who could he possibly know that would be able to help Jason at basketball?

But by dinner the next night, he'd forgotten about it. He had just started following Kaiya on Instagram, and by the time he looked up from her feed, it was already 8:25pm. "Crap!" He grabbed his basketball and rushed out the door. When he arrived at the address, he was confused. It was an even worse basketball court than the one he usually went to. It looked ancient, like it hadn't been touched in a decade. A few flickering lights buzzed over the cracked pavement.

The court was empty, except for one person: a very tall man, shooting free throws. Jason approached, out of breath. "Hi, I'm Jason. Sorry I'm late."

The man turned, and Jason's mouth dropped open. <u>Standing in front of him was none other than T.D.</u>, the same legendary man who just a few weeks ago had thrilled him with his "Pound the Stone" speech at sales training.

"Jason, I'm T.D." He shook Jason's hand, unblinking.

Jason's mind sped, as he stammered, "So... how do you know Russ?"

"Russell? Oh, we're old friends. He has helped me with a few things." Jason nodded, still confused. T.D. gestured to the court. "You're wondering why we're here? When I first moved to this city, I worked out almost every night here. It was the only quiet court I could find. Plus, having too many resources can actually be detrimental sometimes. That's one reason why most of the world's talent hotbeds never have the best resources or training facilities."[4]

"Oh... cool." It didn't make much sense to Jason, but he wasn't about to argue.

"Look, Jason. Russell said you needed help on your game, and I was looking forward to giving you that. But you got here at 8:36."

---

4 *The Talent Code*, by Daniel Coyle

"But… that's just a few minutes late!"

"And you lost the opportunity to work out with me tonight. *Life and basketball are determined by inches. Lots of small, seemingly insignificant things, that added up and compounded over time will determine the trajectory of your life.* Most people focus on all the big stuff, failing to realize it is the little stuff that makes all the difference. Just ask Napoleon."

"The French emperor?"

"The same one. If it weren't for one very important 'little thing,' you and I might be speaking French right now instead of English. Do you want to know why? Because of nails." He chuckled at Jason's confusion. "Napoleon's downfall was losing the battle of Waterloo. But what most people don't realize is that he would have won it except that his men forgot to bring the headless nails to hammer into the British cannons to turn them into useless hunks of bronze. So instead, the British regained the cannons and defeated the French.[5] In the big scheme of things, nails are just a little thing, but as I hope you are learning, the little things often determine the outcome."

"Don't worry, I won't leave you with nothing. Here." T.D. pulled a neatly-folded piece of paper from his pocket and handed it to Jason. "This is the workout we were going to go through."

When Jason looked up from the paper, T.D. was gone. Vanishing like a ghost. Jason was rattled. He couldn't believe it. Inches? He respected T.D., but he was sure it was talent and money that determine the trajectory of people's lives, not inches.

And the workout? What a joke! It was a bunch of basic drills Jason did as a kid, playing at the YMCA. He was embarrassed even reading it. So as he walked off, he threw the paper in the trash.

---

5 *The Little Things,* by Andy Andrews

# CHAPTER 11

# FOCUS ON YOUR STRENGTHS

THE NEXT NIGHT, Russ was still away. When Jason asked Jan why, she just smiled. "Sometimes his work takes him elsewhere." It didn't make any sense to Jason, but he didn't want to offend her so he kept it to himself. Plus, he was more interested in how Russ knew T.D. in the first place.

"Oh, they've known each other for years. I think they met after a game at the stadium one night," Jan said nonchalantly.

And the next night, when Russ was back, he didn't reveal much more. He just asked Jason how their training had gone. Jason was worried about his reaction when he told Russ that he'd been late, but the older man didn't seem surprised. "Well, at least you got something from it."

"Not really. I threw the workout away. I mean it's so simple I have it memorized, but there's no way he does it! It was just some simple drills, and a ton of footwork stuff. I'm already great at footwork. That workout was too basic. He must not realize how good I am."

Russ let out a deep sigh. "Jason, for all our instant access to high-level knowledge, we often overlook the value of 'basic.' And for all our obsession with innovation, we often miss the power in doing the unremarkable with incredible consistency. For example, take an experiment by nine Michigan hospitals in 2004. Everyone was looking for ways to save more lives, reduce infections, and save money. Turns out this experiment did all of the above. In less than 18 months, they had saved over 1,500 lives, reduced infections by 66%, and saved over $75 million dollars. The experiment they did had nothing to do with innovation though. In fact it was an exercise so basic it was almost laughable. It was just a checklist of five simple things everyone did before entering the operating room. The first thing on it? *Wash your hands.*"

Jason's eyes widened, as he realized this reminded him of T.D.'s talk about "inches." Russ went on, "Just because we know we should do something, doesn't mean we do it, and it definitely doesn't mean we do it every single time. *We often get caught up seeking the remarkable, instead of doing the unremarkable with remarkable consistency.*"

For the next week, Jason did just that, keeping up with the simple routine. But if he were honest with himself, he just felt stupid doing it. He had moved on to more elaborate workouts years ago. Following the simple fundamental drills TD had written on the paper felt limiting, so the next week he only did it half the time. The other half, he began working on his shooting with his left hand.

At dinner one night, Russ noticed Jason flexing his left hand. "Doing some shooting?"

"Yeah." Jason shrugged it off. "I need to even it out. Once the cast comes off, my right hand is going to need a lot of rehab, so I need to work out my left in the mean time."

Russ nodded his head, "Hmmmm, interesting."

"You disagree? I thought for sure you'd be excited about me working on my weaknesses instead of my strengths."

Russ let out a little laugh, "Earlier in my life I would have. But over time, I've become a bigger believer in the opposite: *going all in on your strengths.*

A researcher named Marcus Buckingham conducted interviews with thousands of the best business managers in the world, and what his research found is that you grow the most in the areas of your strength.[6] So while I know you might have heard otherwise all your life, I think that if you focus on your weaknesses, you simply become average at a lot of things, but the master of none. Mastery is hard and it takes a lot of time, effort, and energy. So if you have limited components of each of those, you should probably spend the majority of your time on your strengths and then maybe fifteen to twenty percent of your time on managing your weaknesses."

"Did you know that John Wooden, the guy who won ten National Championships at UCLA, never scouted the other team? His teams focused only on developing their own strengths, and let their opponents worry about stopping them."

Jason was impressed. "I didn't know that. I can't see Coach Michael agreeing! He talks all the time about developing our weaknesses, and we watch hours of scout film to prep."

"Well, I'm not your coach, but if I were you, this summer I would focus more on doing the dirty hard work that most people won't do. What would you say is your greatest strength?"

"I probably like shooting the most, but people have always said my footwork is what makes me so hard to guard. But I hate working on it. It's boring, and plus, I'm already good at it."

Russ nodded, "I get that, but I can tell you that there aren't very many players in the country, no less the state, who are going to do basic footwork drills every single day with the discipline and focus of a world class

---

6 *First, Break All The Rules,* by Marcus Buckingham and Curt Coffman

surgeon. Not many kids are going to study the footwork of the greats and watch their highlight films to deliberately take in their footwork every day. But I know that if you do that – something that is easy to do, but easier not to do – it will make a massive difference over time. Most people overlook the basics and the 'boring.' They might be willing to work hard, but rarely are they actually willing to do the hard work. *There is a big difference between just working hard, and actually being disciplined enough to do the hard work.*"

Jason nodded, thinking that over as he excused himself for bed.

# CHAPTER 12

## MAINTAINING THE MASK

THE NEXT NIGHT, Jason got a call from his aunt just as he finished work. She told him that Jason's mother had strained her back lifting something heavy at work and was recuperating at home. Jason was alarmed, "Is she okay?"

"Yes, the doctors said she'll be just fine, but she'll have to take two weeks off of work. I just thought you should know, since she would never tell you this herself. She's worried you'll come back to take care of her, the silly woman."

"Because I will!" Jason was already thinking about the next bus he could catch to make it back home, but his aunt cut him off.

"You really don't need to, Jason. We'll take good care of her, she will be okay."

As much as she reassured him, Jason was rattled by the news. While he was happy his mom was okay, he knew that even one missed week of work would cost her lost hours and pay, since she worked nights as a waitress and relied on tips. He felt terrible for being away from her, but he also knew that if he wanted to help offset the costs he could only do it by selling more books. He felt trapped.

He was silent during dinner, and was looking forward to getting away to the basketball courts. But Russ stopped him on the porch, asking him point-blank what was going on. When Jason told him, he was concerned, but not just for Jason's mother. "How are you doing, Jason?"

Jason shrugged it off, doing his best to stay strong. "I'm fine, honestly."

"Are you sure about that?" Russ pushed back.

"Yeah, I said I'm fine, stop asking!" Jason snapped.

He was angry that Russ kept pushing. But Russ wasn't rattled. He just set his book down. "Jason, is it okay if I ask you a very difficult question?"

Jason just shrugged, still angry. "What…"

"That guy you punched in the big game, the one that landed you here. Why did you hit him?"

Thinking about that just made Jason angrier. "He was holding my wrist so I couldn't block his shot when he drove, giving me elbows and taking cheap shots. You play like that against me, you're not getting away with it."

"Why not?"

Jason shifted, defensive. "What do you mean 'why not'? Because if you let someone do that to you, they don't respect you!"

Russ nodded, musing. "Okay, so it was about respect then? Not basketball?"

"Sure, if you want to look at it that way. But you can't just let people walk all over you, on the court or off."

"Why not?"

Jason could feel his blood rising. "Are you serious? Because you lose face. You know that!"

"Oh, I do. But I call it something else, Jason." Russ's eyes grew clear and intense. "I don't call it 'not losing face.' I call it 'maintaining the mask,' and it's the same reason you won't be honest with me about how worried you really are about your mom right now."

Jason shifted uncomfortably, not knowing what to say. Russ went on, "Our culture has taught you that as a young man, you can never authentically show any feeling other than anger. Unfortunately, anger is a secondary emotion. It always comes from something else. But showing anything else is seen as weakness. So your two choices are to be seen as weak, or to get angry. Does that sound about right?"

Jason nodded, thinking back to all the fights he'd been in, and the anger that had pretty much always been a part of him.

Russ continued, "And so you put a mask over it, and you fight to keep it in place. But here's the irony. Putting a mask over weakness doesn't make you strong, Jason. It just makes you a liar. Your conscience knows the difference, and it won't let you get away with it. And so over time, those lies you tell the world about yourself become a prison, one that won't let you ever tell the truth about who you are, and what you truly feel. But no one can stop themselves from feeling things, and if you can't let yourself talk about what you feel, it builds up inside you. And with enough time and pressure, that can blow up, sometimes with tragic results."

Jason didn't want to believe this was true, though he somehow intuitively knew deep down in his gut that it was. Russ was hitting on something big here, but the more he knew it, the more he resisted it.

Russ seemed to sense it, continuing, "Whether we like it or not, we all wear a mask each day. It's the face we show the world, but it often isn't our most authentic self. For many years, I wore the mask of a strong, successful guy who had everything in his life together, but it was a lie. I fought and I hustled, but I couldn't stop life from ripping it off. It almost took my life being taken from me to force me to throw my mask away and live my life authentically."

Then, abruptly, he locked eyes with Jason. "What masks do you wear, Jason?"

"Um, I don't know..." Jason scoffed, shrugging it off. "I don't really even think I have one. I just usually try to be myself I guess."

"So, no mask?" Jason nodded, and Russ raised an eyebrow. "Interesting. Could you tell me about your father?"

Jason froze up, something deep inside him snapping shut. He felt the familiar heat of anger prickle on his neck and narrowed his eyes at Russ. "No. That's off limits."

But if he expected Russ to keep pushing, he was wrong. The older man just nodded, "I respect that, Jason. I was just making a point. Maybe it's worth thinking about."

Everything in Jason wanted Russ to be wrong, but that night he couldn't sleep. He sat awake in bed for a long time, thinking about what Russ had said. He had always tried to not talk about his dad, even though he never quite knew why. He just knew that it was kind of a locked door in his heart, something he had agreed with himself that he would never open.

# CHAPTER 13

# PRISON

"I JUST DON'T get it," Jason said as he ended a call on his phone. "Some people are so locked into the wrong way of doing things."

"How so?" Russ asked. As usual, they were sitting out on the porch watching the sun set.

"Well, I asked one of my buddies from the team if he wanted to swing by to hang out for a day and see what it's like to grind door-to-door, but he said he can't do it because he is tired from work. Do you know where he works? A fast-food place! For a boss that he hates, doing a job that he hates. And look, I don't always love selling books, but at least I'm working for myself! And I think it might be something he'd be good at, maybe he could do it next summer."

Russ chuckled, "Conditioning is a powerful sedative, Jason. I remember watching a really powerful stage drama one time about a group of people who were trapped inside a prison for many years. Eventually though, the prison doors were unlocked and the armed guards had abandoned their posts, but because of years of conditioning the prisoners refused to leave. A man came to visit them, pleading with them to go, but they chastised him and drove him away. I think the same thing has happened in our culture. All the rules have changed, and there is no reason to stay trapped in a job you hate, but for most people in our culture, that's really hard to believe."

Jason thought that was odd coming from a street sweeper. "What do you mean?"

"Well, it's hard to believe you could just walk away from prison and pursue your dreams and destiny. Most people would rather believe someone else is keeping them chained up than accept the truth: the only one responsible for keeping us where we are, is us. Everyone has challenges. Some see them as an excuse but the rare few choose to see them for what they really are: the forging ground for greatness.

When you've been stuck in prison for most of your life, it is hard to believe that the world is full of endless opportunities. But our world is no longer a prison: it's a meritocracy. The internet, social media, and amazing advancements in technology have made it possible for anyone who is willing to pound the stone and willing to consistently hit publish to reach the entire world.

Does it help if you have a huge budget and fancy degrees? To some extent it might, but it's no longer a legitimate excuse. All over the world people are realizing that if they make amazing art, do incredible work, and pound the stone persistently, that anything is possible.

The gatekeepers no longer wield the same power that they did for hundreds of years. No matter your race, gender, sexual preferences, family background, or anything else, those who do the best work, make the best art, and have the best ideas, will rise to the top. Those who care enough to truly connect, who are courageous enough to persistently hit publish on whatever they create, and who pound the stone in spite of failures and setbacks, will win the long game.

But the hard truth is this: no one can let you out of prison. You, and you alone, must choose to leave. Most people never will. Most people will choose the three square meals per day and the comfortable structure of a scheduled life, even if it is killing their potential. They prefer certainty over the wide-open, uncharted culture of the internet, social media, and a constantly shifting landscape of new technologies. Because as you've experienced, the world of pounding the stone isn't always easy, and is rarely, if ever, comfortable."

Jason nodded, "You've got that right! Still, I feel bad for my buddy. He really should get out of that job. Especially after hearing you talk about this stuff..."

"I'll give you a word of warning on that, and I know this from personal experience." Russ shook his head, "A wise friend of mine once said: '*If someone insists they need to be in prison even though the door is unlocked, then I am not going to argue. They are free to stay in prison.*'" [7]

Jason thought about those words as he grabbed his ball and headed to the courts. They made sense, but they also made him sad when he thought about all the people he knew who worked in jobs they hated when they could quit at any moment. He determined that he would do his best to keep pounding the stone with relentless persistence, so that that would never be him. It was so weird hearing Russ talk about stuff like this considering his own job, but the one thing Jason started to realize the more time he spent with Russ and Jan was that they had the two things people truly want in life: *peace and contentment in abundance*. He knew he wanted those things in his life as well.

---

7 James Altucher

## CHAPTER 14

# STOP COUNTING

As THE WEEKS passed, Jason got used to the rhythm of life as a door to door salesman. Well, as used to it as a stubborn teenager could. "Pound the stone" was more like, *feet pounded by stone.* It was by far the hardest work he'd ever done. To be honest, most of the time he just tried to get through it.

He hoped he'd be able to figure out how to sell better as the time passed so his numbers would go up. But that wasn't happening. Five books here, seven or eight there. He still had yet to get anywhere close to his record of fifty-five from his first day. What was he doing wrong?

"Did you take up coloring?" Jan said to Jason as she walked into the living room. He was filling in a colored chart.

"No, it's my sales chart... and it says I'm behind schedule." Whenever he got discouraged, he thought of that chart. Every line he marked was one more step toward making it back on the team. But instead of inspiring Jason, the chart had started to depress him. Any day he didn't make a mark, or made only a tiny one, it just reminded him that he was failing. The number at the top – 1,200 – seemed further away as each day passed. But the more he obsessed over it, the worse he felt about his performance and the more his process suffered.

One night as Jason came back from basketball practice, Russ was reading out on the porch as usual. "Looking a little tired, son. What's going on?"

Jason collapsed into a porch chair, defeated. "People aren't buying books, and it's stupid that I have to sell so many. It's already a couple weeks into the summer and I'm way behind my goal. I need to sell 100 books a week, but right now I'm only at 95 total."

Russ got a gleam in his eye. "Hmm. You want to make more sales, right?"

"Yeah."

"Then stop counting them."

"What?!" Jason couldn't believe what he was hearing.

Russ looked at Jason with empathy as he recognized that same ambition in himself. Ambition that had almost derailed him at many points along his own journey. "Jason, one of the wisest things I've learned is that with your eyes on the goal, you have no eyes for the journey. I understand that you think you know where you want to get to, but it's the process that gets us there. It's all the little things. When you focus on every thing other than your journey, you are more likely to get lost and end up far from your desired destination."

Jason was trying to follow, but it was really hard. He didn't get it. "I'm not sure I understand."

Russ motioned to Jason's phone. "Pull up YouTube and type in, 'Inky Johnson.' I want to show you something T.D. sent me earlier today." As Jason obeyed, he went on, "Inky was a lock-down cornerback playing football at the University of Tennessee and was slated to be a lottery pick in the upcoming NFL draft, but late in his junior year he had a freak injury during a routine tackle that almost killed him and left one of his arms paralyzed."

Russ clicked play on the video. Jason watched, mesmerized, as Inky spoke...

> *"So I have been intrigued with, can you be committed to the process of what you do without being emotionally attached to the result of what you do? Because a lot of people can be committed to the process of what they do if the results don't change. But the moment the result or the outcome changes of what they are chasing, they shut it down or they quit simply because the result changed. So can we be committed to the process of what we do but not emotionally to the result of what we do? Understanding everyday I get up and give everything I got to everything I am a part of simply because this is who I am. Like, the only thing I need every day is 86,400 seconds. I don't need some reward to chase. I don't need some reward. The only thing I need is breath in my body and I'm going to flat out go and get it!"*[8]

Jason felt goosebumps cover his body. He was blown away by Inky. He nodded to Russ, "I didn't recognize his name at first, but I remember seeing his story on *ESPN* the other day! I think I finally understand what you want me to do."

"Good," Russ nodded. "But before you go to bed, you need to know how it works."

---

8 *All I Need*, by Inky Johnson, clip available on his Instagram page.

# CHAPTER 15

## 1%

"Are you sure?" Jason asked, confused. He thought it was pretty obvious how it worked.

"Well, I know how badly you want to hit your sales goal, and I know you want to see exponential growth this summer. But let me tell you about how that growth actually works. It happens 1% at a time, and that's a lot faster than you think."

"Really? What do you mean?"

"Back in 2010, a guy named Dave Brailsford was tasked with a serious challenge. He had just taken over England's cycling team, a team that had never won a Tour de France. Dave had a unique strategy though. Rather than focusing on big goals like winning a Tour de France, he was going to focus on improving the little things – everything from the way the team washed their hands, all the way to the type of pillow they slept on– by just 1%. He believed that if they could just improve everything by 1%, then through the power of small aggregated gains they should be able to win the Tour De France in five years." [9]

Jason leaned forward, hooked. "So, did he do it?"

---

9 James Clear article, *This Coach Improved Every Tiny Thing by 1 Percent and Here's What Happened*

"No. Turns out, Dave was wrong: they won it in just three years." Russ grinned as Jason laughed. *"We want big sexy gains, but there is much more power in the small, dirty, and unsexy marginal gains added up and compounded over time. Don't fall for the trap everyone else does. Focus on pounding the stone and finding all those little improvements, and trust the process."*

Something about what Russ said finally started to make some sense for Jason, but he still didn't want to believe it. How could you possibly accomplish more by totally forgetting about your goal? That went against everything he'd ever been taught, in school or sports or life.

So, in spite of the inner voice that told him he should maybe listen to Russ, he chose to tune it out. Russ was just a street sweeper after all. Jason was sure he could reach his goal by focusing harder on it.

# CHAPTER 16

## YOU, INC.

As the summer wore on however, things only seemed to get worse. Jason's goal kept getting further away, and with each day his heart posture and effort suffered.

He was so confused. He'd always had an easy smile, and found it natural to charm people, but none of that was working now. Door after door slammed in his face, no matter how wide he smiled or how hard he tried to connect with people. Nothing was working.

Finally, after a week without a single sale, Jason stopped trying. He slept through his alarm, finally getting up mid-afternoon. As he poured himself a bowl of cereal in the kitchen, Jan walked in with a stack of mail. She didn't seem surprised to see him.

"Good morning, Jason. Are you feeling okay? You're not sick?" He shook his head, crunching cereal. "Then why aren't you out selling books?"

He shrugged. "It's pointless. I can't sell any. Nothing is working, and I've tried everything!"

"Everything? Are you sure about that?" The gleam in her eyes stopped him from responding. "I guess focusing on your goal hasn't really been working out for you, huh?" She tried to hide her chuckle. "Russ told me he didn't think you had really listened to his advice about the process."

Jason felt a flash of anger. "It's not like I haven't been trying!"

"You know, Yoda said; 'there is only *do* or *do not*, there is no try'. Better question though, is, have you consistently given your very best?" The way she said it made Jason stop and really wonder. "Look, Jason. At one time in my life, I also sold products door to door, just like you. Except I sold phone book advertising to businesses door to door. And what I learned is that sales are more about the little things than the big ones."

Jason shook his head in total frustration. "The little things? Everyone keeps talking about the little things. But guess what, I need BIG things to happen if I'm going to get back on the team!"

"Well, Jason, as my mom always liked to ask me in moments like these, *'How's your strategy working out for you?'*"

Jason's anger melted to defeat, and he let out a big sigh. "Not well...."

Jan looked at him with empathy, "Well, if you would like I could share some of the little things I found helpful?"

Jason brightened up a little bit, "Yes, ma'am, I would appreciate that."

Jan smiled. "Well, the most important little thing is one that takes place internally, and it's your heart posture. Are you there to give or to get? Are you there to close a sale, or to give someone an opportunity to learn something that could change their life?

Did you know that over 90% of human communication is non-verbal? Things like our clothing, body language, facial expressions, and heart posture are communicating long before our mouths are forming words. And our brains are wired to instantly judge and pick up on unconscious cues. It takes your brain just 1/15$^{th}$ of a second to read a micro-expression on someone else's face. So all those non-verbals tell the world a story long before you speak. The best part, though, is that we can always change the story we are telling."

Jason was intrigued. "Huh. I never thought about it like that..."

"The truth is, Jason, the world will only take you as seriously as you take yourself. Until you take yourself seriously, how can you expect anyone else to take you seriously? Be honest with me, would <u>you</u> buy a book from you right now? Do you trust you? Are you dressed like someone you can trust? Do you speak like someone you would trust?"

Jason fell silent as her questions rolled around in his mind. "Here, maybe this is a better way to sum it up. Would you hire yourself for a $250,000 a year job right now?"

Jason looked defeated as the reality sunk in, but Jan went on, encouraging, "Jason, if you saw yourself the way I do, then you would use your time radically differently. You would treat people radically differently. *Until you take yourself seriously, no one else is going to. When you see yourself for who you truly are, and who you were created to be, you will understand the immense power you hold.*"

She looked at the young man in front of her with empathy, and encouraged him. "Look Jason, this is something a lot of people don't figure out until much later in life, so don't be disheartened. I want you to start thinking about yourself as a publicly traded stock. YOU, Inc. *Jason, Inc.* Every choice you make, all those little inches, will determine the price of your stock."

Jason nodded, trying to wrap his mind around it. "Yes, that makes sense."

With a gleam in her eye, Jan prodded him, "And you know, it might help to actually crack open a few of those books you're selling. I've read most of them, and they're really good. It might even help drive that stock price up a little bit!"

Jason blushed. How did she know he hadn't read any of them?

# CHAPTER 17

# A WEALTH OF WISDOM

ALL AFTERNOON, JASON couldn't stop thinking about what Jan had said. He thought he really was taking this seriously, but after talking to her, he knew he wasn't. She was right. He wouldn't hire himself for a $250,000 a year job. Honestly, he might not even hire himself for a $25,000 a year job. He knew he needed to start investing in himself and taking himself seriously.

Halfway through the afternoon, he stopped off at a restaurant for a cold drink. As he took his break, he looked through the books in his backpack. Just like practice, he had always hated reading. He avoided it if he could, always using *Cliffs Notes* or just looking up a summary online. But it seemed that this time, he couldn't avoid it.

So he decided to start with the first book, *The Slight Edge*.

It started out easily enough, and the more he read it, the more interested he got. He tried to not focus on the fact that reading this book was like talking to Russ, at certain points it felt like Russ might have been a ghostwriter for the book.

By the time Jason looked up from the book to check his phone, he couldn't believe it; he'd been sitting there for two hours! That had never happened before. And it wasn't just because he knew that this would help his sales. He had to admit that he really, actually liked the book.

It made a lot of sense to him. He had heard of compound interest before, but he never realized that it worked for everything in life, not just savings accounts. It made a lot of sense for basketball. He knew a lot of the best players built their game on doing boring things really well, things that, like the book said, were "easy to do, easier not to do." Things like layups or free throws. Sometimes those fundamentals really did make the difference between a win and a loss.

Jason left the restaurant buzzing with energy and curiosity. That night, after helping Jan with the dishes, he sat out on the porch next to Russ and kept reading. Russ just grinned, proud.

For the rest of the week, Jason couldn't stop. He burned through each book on the list, devouring them like a starving person at a buffet. Each had fascinating stories with timeless wisdom, and he filled a whole notebook with notes while reading. By the end of the week, he felt like his brain would burst into flames. It was full of so much new information! Now he just had to put it to use.

# CHAPTER 18

## GRIT

"Cut it off." Jason closed his eyes as he pointed the barber's scissors at his mohawk. It was time he took himself seriously, and the mohawk wasn't helping, so it had to go.

Later that night, Russ smiled as Jason got home. "Looking good! What made you decide to change hairstyles?" Jason shot a look at Jan, and he laughed, as Russ declared, "I thought so. Let me guess, she gave you the YOU, Inc. speech?"

"How did you know?"

"Hey, do you think you're the first one she used that on?" Russ shook his head and laughed.

"I have to admit, I think it worked. I actually wanted to ask you, Russ, would it be okay if I borrow a nice shirt or two for work? I think it might help me look a little more professional than this..." He nodded to his baggy basketball shorts and big t-shirt covered in loud graphics.

"Of course! Come on." Lucky for Jason, Russ had plenty of old clothes, and he and Jason were roughly the same size. He gave Jason a half-dozen shirts and two pairs of slacks to try on.

Jason was surprised how stylish and fitted everything was. Certainly felt strange for a street sweeper to have. But he didn't complain. Jan was right – even if he didn't quite recognize himself, he definitely looked much more professional.

That night, he cut his practice session short to write out a new pitch for each book he had read that included personal stories about what he learned from each. It was hard, but he remembered the principle of the *Slight Edge* – "easy to do, easier not to do" – and kept going. He even practiced each pitch before bed. It felt silly, but as he finished, he felt more confident than ever.

But by lunch the next day, he was ready to give up. He didn't sell a single book. All his extra effort seemed to be for nothing, and he felt like a total failure. Still, he knew that quitting was no longer an option. He wasn't playing with one eye on the scoreboard anymore.

Before knocking on each door, he reminded himself: *find common ground and focus on what you can give, not what you can get.*

And sure enough, at his last stop of the day, it finally happened. After they finished their conversation, the man he was talking to smiled and said, "Sounds great! I'm in!" Jason walked away with a spring in his step. He'd finally broken his losing streak!

But by the end of the week, the spring was gone and doubt had set in. He was quiet and angry by the time he made it back to the house. He didn't say anything all the way through dinner, either. It was the first time he had refused to answer Jan's patented four nightly questions:

> *What are you grateful for?*
> *What was the best failure you had today?*
> *What did you do well?*
> *If you could do today over again, what would you do differently?*

He went to bed that night exhausted and woke up to the smell of coffee and bacon. Jan was cooking up breakfast in the kitchen, putting together the ingredients to a big breakfast dish.

"Could you help me with the peppers, Jason? Nice and small, please." She handed him a knife, and he got to work. As he did, she asked him point-blank, "So, this week was a tough one?"

He nodded, "Yes, ma'am. I sold one book per day this week, that's it."

Jan just smiled. "You know Jason, that might not seem like much. But a wise man once said, 'One is greater than zero.'[10] In fact, one long term research project published by Harvard found that the greatest predictor of future success in life is the ability to delay gratification. The word I like to describe that ability is the one my friend Angela uses: *grit*. She calls it the passion and endurance to keep working towards one's mission despite setbacks and failures. And especially good for you, she found that those who experienced more setbacks and failure on their journey, but persisted anyway, often ended up better because of it."[11]

Jason snorted, unconvinced. But Jan pressed on, "Let me ask you a question Jason. Has basketball come pretty naturally to you, or have you had to move from failure to failure without losing enthusiasm?"

Jason took a deep breath as he thought about it, "Before this summer? Everything came really naturally to me, but it feels like all of that is gone now."

"Awesome! I'm so glad to hear that!" Jan said with too much joy for Jason's liking.

---

10  Gary Vee quote.

11  *Grit*, by Angela Duckworth

"Why would you ever say something like that?" Jason couldn't hide his disdain.

"Oh, I'll tell you why Jason, because even though we have an obsession with 'naturals' and 'talent' in our society, those people always end up worse off in the long run if they never learn to develop grit. We get distracted and enamored by people who seem to have the "it" factor, instead of putting in the dirty, hard work to develop what really determines whether you fulfill your potential in life: *grit*. The only way you can really develop grit is by experiencing failures and setbacks. Quite frankly, the fact that you are learning this now in a safe environment with people like Russ and I that are going to keep encouraging you and supporting you to persevere is much better than experiencing it once you get to college or the pros. Wouldn't you rather experience it now and start developing your grit muscles? I've heard some of the college and pro coaches can be quite tough!"

"Yeah, I guess so. It just sucks. Failing sucks."

"It sure does, but guess what, the person who has mastered their craft has failed many more times than the beginner has even tried. The path to mastery will never be easy or without repeated setbacks and failures." Jason nodded as she finished up the breakfast dish, mixing the chopped peppers. It looked heavenly, and smelled even better.

Jan saw his hungry eyes and smiled. "Take this dish, for example. You could make a faster, cheaper version of it by buying it frozen and popping it in the microwave. Or, you could do what I did, and master making it on your own from the very best ingredients, even if you fail the first hundred times. *There is no such thing as microwaveable mastery.* Greatness comes just like a good meal, with time, patience, and love. And if you don't believe me, take a bite of this!"

Jason was more than happy to oblige, and Jan was right, the dish was amazing!

# CHAPTER 19

## SIDES TO A BOX

"Dang, you look like a totally different guy!" Travis stood at Russ and Jan's door, looking at Jason in his slacks and button-down shirt. He couldn't believe the transformation.

"Yeah," Jason nodded. "I feel different, too. Hopefully it's a good thing."

Travis grinned, "You do look better without a mohawk. C'mon, let's go sell some books!"

Travis was spending the day with Jason after being away at a summer academic training program for high-achieving high school students. It was held at an Ivy League college, and all summer Jason had seen the highlights from Travis's Instagram: days at the lake on jet ski's, tours of New York City hotspots, even a charity golf tournament where Travis played with NBA players.

Jason thought the two of them couldn't have had more different summers, but Travis seemed like he couldn't be happier to be there, going door to door with Jason. He even jumped in and helped sell a few books, thanks to his contagious personality.

That evening, they punched out early to get in some time on the court together. After a summer of mostly solo practice, it felt great to play with Travis, and Jason was reminded how much he loved the energy and action of playing with a teammate. They finished the workout sweaty, tired, and happy, and walked back to Russ and Jan's in the humid air as the sun set.

Travis smiled, dribbling the ball. "Man, I forgot how fun ball can be! I needed this. I've been putting in too many hours studying."

"For that college prep thing?"

"Yeah. It's supposed to basically guarantee that you go to the school of your choice. It's just... a lot of work. Lot of pressure." He sighed, waving it off. "Nothing like this. I mean that in a good way. You've got a really good thing going this summer."

"What?! Are you kidding? This summer sucks!"

"I don't know about that. Seems to me that you really like what you're doing. And then you get to hang out with Russ and Jan for dinner, then go play ball at night? Sounds perfect to me."

"Perfect?! This is the opposite of perfect, trust me. I haven't had a day off all summer! And don't tell me I've got a 'perfect' summer when you're the one who's going to the lake and getting to golf with NBA players! If anyone's having a perfect summer this year, it's you!"

Travis reddened, like he was embarrassed. He mumbled, "Those are just pictures, man."

"So what? I'd still rather be doing that than what I'm doing. Plus, at least you know you have a spot waiting for you back on the team!"

"Hey, after what I've seen today? You got this, buddy." Travis shot Jason an encouraging smile, as they turned into Russ's driveway. They looked up to find Russ, standing in front of a massive cardboard box. He lit up when he saw them, "Perfect timing, gentlemen. Can you help me haul this to the back yard?"

Jason and Travis picked it up, waddling into the backyard. They set the box down with a thick THUMP! Jason looked at it curiously, "What is this thing?"

"This is a *Traeger Grill*, grills the best steaks in the country! How was practice?"

"He's rusty," Jason joked, nodding to Travis. "He's been too busy having the perfect summer to pick up a ball!"

Travis shrugged it off, but Russ noticed him get quiet, so he said: "It's funny, you know. 'Perfect' means very different things, depending on who you ask."

"What do you mean?"

"Let me ask you a question: how many sides does this box have?" He pointed to the grill box.

Jason and Travis exchanged looks, then counted the box's sides. "Six. Obviously."

Russ just turned up an eyebrow, "Are you sure?"

"Yes!" Jason shook his head. "Travis is like the second-ranked person in our class. We're sure."

Russ sighed, "Well, you were close. The box actually has twelve sides: there is a front side and a back side to each of those six sides you said it has."

Jason groaned and shot Travis a look, "I'm sorry, he does this all the time. Trick questions and stuff." He turned back to Russ, who was still smiling. "So what's your point?"

Russ laughed, "The point is that in life we often forget that what we see isn't always all there is, and that there are always more sides to everything and everyone. Every person and every event in our lives is multi-dimensional. Just because we aren't aware of them, doesn't mean those sides don't exist.

But here is the really important point: we make decisions and our reality is influenced by our perception and our perspective, not by the thing itself. There is always another side to consider, another perspective to consider, and when you start to understand this it opens your mind up to an amazing world of possibilities.

But if you close your mind off to alternative perspectives, then you will never be able to see or benefit from them. As soon as you form a strong opinion about something, you immediately start shutting your mind off to seeing other possibilities. It's not that they don't exist, it's just that you will have extreme difficulty seeing them even if they're right in front of your face.

And look, I was your age once too. So I know it's tempting to think that you know it all already, and that old people like me don't understand your world. And yes, sometimes that is true, but other times it's not. The next time you're facing a tough situation remember this box and that there are always more sides than you might see upon first glance. What you see in your environment is not reality, it is simply your perception of reality. If you are open to changing your perspective, you might find an amazing reality has been awaiting you, *in your exact same environment.* The same way that to a three-year-old this big box isn't trash, it can be anything from a space ship to a rainforest."

Later that night, as Travis and Jason said goodbye, Jason apologized again. "Russ is so weird sometimes. He's got a lot of opinions for a street sweeper."

Travis looked surprised, "Russ is a street sweeper? He sure doesn't talk like one."

"Yeah, I know. I don't get it either." The friends said goodbye, and Travis wished Jason well on his remaining weeks.

"See you soon, man. And don't worry: it'll be over before you know it, and we'll be back on the court together."

# CHAPTER 20

# PERSISTENCE

It TURNED OUT that Jan's advice about grit made sense for more than just Jason's summer job.

While his days were filled with pounding the stone in his business and on the court, his quiet moments were often filled with something else: Kaiya. He couldn't get her out of his mind. But she didn't respond to any of his messages on Instagram, and even though she wasn't very active anyway, it made Jason wonder what he was doing wrong.

One night after dinner, Jan spotted him scrolling through her feed. When he admitted that it was a girl he liked who wouldn't give him the time of day, she just chuckled. "Well, just because your idea of how to get her attention isn't working, doesn't mean it will never happen. Tell me about her. What is she interested in?"

Jason nodded, and he remembered that book she was reading, *Hustle*. That was it! He ordered it on Amazon, and started reading it immediately when it showed up.

He couldn't help but smile at a chapter titled, "There's Always a Back Door." The author talked about how even though he didn't have a sport psychology degree, he still built his business from the ground up by using his career as a D1 college athlete to provide something most sport psychologists never could: the perspective of someone who understood what his clients were going through from personal experience.

"There's always a back door." Those words echoed in Jason's mind as he typed out some notes on the book, and then messaged Kaiya.

*J: You have good taste in books. Just finished that book you were reading, Hustle. It was FIRE!!*

He knew he might not have a prayer to talk to her, but he thought if anything was going to get her attention, it was going to be this. Sure enough, the next morning he had a reply.

*K: It's so good, right?! What was most helpful to you?*

Jason was glad that he'd taken so many notes. He quickly put together a list, and they messaged back and forth for a while before she signed off--

*K: OK gtg. Back to work. Have a new client to meet with.*
*J: Good luck!*
*K: You can keep that luck in your pocket. Haven't you seen Man on Fire? There's only two kinds of people, trained and untrained, and I'm trained. Luck is for people that haven't trained to be clutch. I don't need luck.*

Jason just shook his head. Who was this girl? Nobody talked like that, not even the most over-the-top confident guys he knew. He had never met anyone like this girl, and it drove him nuts that despite wanting to get to know her so badly, she still turned him down left and right.

# CHAPTER 21

## "WHAT DO YOU KNOW?"

THE WEEKS PASSED, and while Jason was making more sales, he started to worry.

With only a few weeks left in the summer, he wasn't sure he was going to make his goal. He had followed Russ's advice and hadn't "checked the scoreboard" in weeks. Instead, he just kept pushing, no matter how tired he got. He tried to keep doing the 'little things' in both sales and training, and "surrender the outcome." But when his curiosity finally got too strong and he actually checked his sales numbers, his heart hit the floor... the total was only 689.

*How could that be true?* All those days spent sweating and hauling that stupid backpack full of books through every street in the city... 689 books was all he had to show for it? All he could think about was how stupid he was for listening to Russ. This whole time he should have been doing things his own way, not listening to some old street sweeper.

And that night after dinner, he told him as much. "I've tried everything you told me to do! None of it works! There's no way I'm going to make my numbers in just a couple weeks!"

Russ listened quietly. "Trust the process, Jason. It's just that simple. No one achieved greatness and mastered their craft in one summer."

"Greatness!! What do you know about greatness? You sweep streets for a living!! You drive a Subaru!! You sound like you're trying to live vicariously through me and the other kids you've hosted, because you obviously blew your shot at 'greatness'!" He pushed back from the table, boiling, "I'm over this! All of it!" He turned and stormed off to his room to pack his bag.

As he madly threw clothes into a suitcase, Russ walked in. Jason turned his head to try and conceal the angry tears that were starting down his face.

"So this is all it took? You are going to quit now, over this?" Russ shrugged. "Interesting.

You're free to quit. But think about it first. There's a quote that my friend Warren loves, '*the chains of habit are too light to feel until they are too heavy to be broken.*' If you are going to quit on something like this, what are you going to do when things really get hard in life? Like when you have a kid of your own and you want to leave your wife. Are you going to quit then, too?"

That really hit a nerve and Jason could feel the anger building up inside of him. He squeezed his hand, recently released from its cast. The anger made it feel stronger. Russ continued…

"Do what you want. But these are the moments where true grit is developed. These moments when it feels like everything inside of you is screaming to quit. In these moments of inescapable frustration, that is where true grit is built on the path to mastery. This moment is an amazing opportunity to develop the grit you're going to need in crucial moments down the road. I know you think you want to quit, but this choice will impact the rest of your life. Now, I have an offer for you."

Russ paused. Then, sensing that Jason was listening, he continued, "I want you to come with me to Austin tomorrow on a business trip. If you still want to leave after, I'll pay for your ride back home. I have a feeling you'll want to stay though. How does that sound?"

After a moment, Jason nodded. "Sure."

Russ started to walk out and then turned back, "Be ready at 6 a.m. sharp."

When Russ left, Jason called his mom and told her what happened. He didn't want to go to Austin, but no matter how much he begged, she said she wouldn't let him back in her home if he didn't go. "Son, those wonderful people have invested too much in you for you to blow this. Your anger is what got you into this situation to begin with, and I'm not going to bail you out. You don't have to stay there, but you can't come here."

That was that. Like it or not, Jason was going to Austin.

# CHAPTER 22

# AUSTIN

THE NEXT MORNING, they hit the road early. Jason almost didn't recognize Russ. He looked like a different person in cleanly pressed jeans, a fresh pair of Nike's, and a blazer that seemed custom-cut to his silhouette, perfectly draped over a black V-neck. For an old guy, he had style.

When they finally got to Austin, they pulled up to what looked like a huge conference center. "Austin Welcomes SXSW" was spelled out in huge block letters on a massive banner across one of the entrances. But instead of parking out front, they pulled around back to a gate, where two huge security guards were checking vehicles.

A blacked-out Range Rover was in front of them, and a brand new Bentley was behind them. Jason was certain they were in the wrong place. Sure enough, one of the guards just motioned for Russ to turn around. "This is VIP parking. You'll need to park in one of the public lots."

Unfazed, Russ handed the man his license, and Jason watched something strange happen. As soon as they read it, the guards exchanged glances and then *apologized* to Russ, "We're so sorry sir, we didn't recognize you. Your detail will meet you up by the entrance."

They waved the car through instantly. Jason watched in amazement as the Subaru pulled to a stop in yet another secured area, where more security guards with earpieces were scrambling to help them out of the car. Jason couldn't figure it out. They were treating Russ like a king. Why?

But before he could ask any questions, they were waved into what looked like the back halls of a stadium or convention center. Someone dressed in black with a headset held a door open for them, and then two more people approached Russ, talking in hushed voices about lots of details about an event that didn't make much sense to Jason as they walked in.

Then he heard the music. The bass pounded so hard it shook the building. He quickly recognized the song – *Monday to Monday* by Saba, one of his favorite up-and-coming rappers – but he couldn't understand why he was hearing it here. Then, it hit him...

They were backstage. Lights flashed through from the stage, and he could hear a huge crowd on the other side of the curtain. Goosebumps flashed across his skin as the song ended, and applause roared from the crowd.

Suddenly, another person wearing a headset approached Jason, "Your seat is ready, sir."

Before he could say anything, they led him out the side entrance, and he saw maybe the most confusing thing yet: Saba himself walked backstage, and embraced Russ like his own father.

Jason's confusion reached its pitch as he was ushered to a roped-off seat in the front row of what seemed like a cavernous room. He couldn't quite see the size of it, just the thousands of faces, all looking up to the stage, where he read a huge banner: "SXSW." Jason had heard of South By Southwest, but he didn't know that much about it. He thought it was just a tech conference.

Now, Saba was back on stage introducing the keynote speaker. "Yo, you all know him, and I have to give credit where credit is due. This cat is one of the OG hustlers, a guy who's started two different hundred-million-dollar companies, was an early investor in Facebook, Twitter, Snapchat, and Uber, and even though he's retired he is still a mentor to some of the biggest names in business... give it up for my man, Russell Carter!"

The arena exploded with cheers, and Jason's mind froze as the speaker walked out: <u>it was Russ.</u>

# CHAPTER 23

## BUILD WISELY

THE NEXT HOUR was a blur. Jason couldn't believe that for the past two and half months, he hadn't figured out who Russ really was. But a quick Google search gave him the basics.

Russell Carter was a legend in the world of business. He'd built two industry-changing businesses, one in food service and one in advertising, had written several NY Times best-sellers, and had served on the board of almost a dozen Fortune 500 companies. Clearly, Russ had to be a multi, multi-millionaire.

Jason tried to think it through, but it didn't get any clearer. Like the fact that Russ was incredibly wealthy, but also worked as a street sweeper? The fact that Russ knew T.D. like an old friend, but never once name-dropped? Or the fact that Russ and Jan still lived in the smallest house on the block, when Jason knew they could easily afford a palace anywhere? It didn't make sense!

But all of that faded away as Russell began to speak. He was a commanding, electric speaker, who held the whole room's attention in his hand. Jason got lost in his words...

"I want to tell you a story about a friend of mine named Kota. He lived in Japan and designed homes for thirty years, and became a true master of his craft. It wasn't talent that made him great, but his passion and grit. He was always the first in and last out at work, and no matter the obstacle, he always treated every home as if it was his own, and poured his heart and soul into everything he built.

After thirty years, he told his boss that he was retiring. But his boss told him their company had just received a contract to build a home for a very important client and they really wanted him to be the one to build the house. Kota was very frustrated, but after talking with his wife he reluctantly agreed to build this one last house. But he made it very clear this was the last one.

And the difference with this one was obvious: his heart simply wasn't in it. He phoned it in. He showed up late and left early, and didn't put in the care and attention to detail that he normally did. He knew it would be up to code, but he also knew it was far from his best work. He had built homes twenty years ago that were much better. But sure enough, it passed inspection. And in the final project meeting, his boss told him, 'Thank you, Kota! We just have one more thing!'

Kota was really upset by now, because he thought they were going to ask him to build another house. But instead, his boss just gave him a small box with a red ribbon and said, 'We are so grateful for you. Your years of mastery have made our company great. This gift is just a small token of our appreciation.' Kota opened the box, and discovered a set of shiny new keys.

His boss smiled, 'The house is yours! You deserve it!'

And instantly, Kota's heart sank. Because unbeknownst to him, the whole time he had been building his own house. And he of all people knew what that meant."

A powerful silence fell, as Russell continued, "*The truth is, with every decision we make, each and every one of us are building our own house. But unfortunately, most people don't operate this way. In business and in life, most people lack patience, and play the short game instead of the long game. They chase quarterly bottom lines, instead of a lasting legacy. Cutting corners to maximize short-term profits might work for a little bit, but it will always come at the expense of what truly matters: the relationships and consumer trust that build a legacy."*

As far back as Jason could see, heads were nodding, the room on the edge of their seats listening to Russ. He shook his head, overwhelmed by how surreal this experience was.

# CHAPTER 24

# FAILURE

AFTERWARD, JASON FOLLOWED the flow of people exiting into a massive lobby area, which was decked out for a party. Tobe Nwigwe was performing a set on stage, as everyone mingled around tall tables in the soft lighting, discussing the keynote. Jason looked around for Russ, as –

"Jason?" The woman approaching him was warm, well-dressed, and graceful. She introduced herself as Caroline, an old friend of Russ's. "Russ tells me you've been pounding the stone all summer doing door-to-door sales. How's it going so far?"

Jason wasn't quite sure who this woman was and why Russ would have been talking about him to her, but he answered honestly. "Not very good. I'm not even close to my goal."

"What's that?"

"Twelve hundred books."

"Wow! That's definitely a lot, especially for your first summer. Do you know who Sara Blakely is?" He shook his head, and she chuckled, "I guess you've probably never needed any of the products she's created. She founded a company called Spanx at 27 years old, and she became a billionaire from that company over the next decade."

Jason was a bit confused as to what this had to do with him. "Huh. Interesting."

"By itself, it's not interesting at all, but her back story of what she did before she founded Spanx is very interesting. She did door to door sales just like you, selling fax machines."

"What's a fax machine?"

Caroline blinked, then laughed. "Well, I guess you could say it's an early version of a scanner. Anyway, she said something insightful about how that job led to her billion-dollar success."

"What did she say?"

"She said, '*I didn't realize that selling fax machines door-to-door was really laying the groundwork for me to be able to be an inventor and create a product that had never been done before and bring it to market, because doing something like that requires hearing the word 'no' a lot... cold-calling to sell fax machines was an amazing training ground for hearing 'no.' I just learned that there's a formula, you have to go through a certain number of 'no's to get to a 'yes,' so don't let it discourage you.*'"

Jason nodded, sighing. "Well, I certainly have heard a lot of 'no's.'"

Caroline glowed, she seemed genuinely excited about that. "That's fantastic!"

"It sure doesn't feel that way." Jason looked down, ashamed.

"I'm sure Russ has told you too many times to count already, but what this summer is really about is *who you're becoming, not what you're achieving. The character you are building through this process is what is truly important.*"

Jason nodded, but that advice sounded like a foreign language to him. Caroline noticed, and went on, "Let me ask you something: if you were to fall short of your sales goal, what would that be?"

"Failing."

"Which would make you what?"

"Uh… a failure."

Caroline's eyes filled with compassion. "Jason, you couldn't be more wrong. Our culture has gotten so confused about what failure really is. The truth is, failing does not make you a failure. Why? <u>Failure is an event, not an identity</u>. Would you consider Babe Ruth a failure?"

"What?! No way, he's one of the greatest baseball players of all time!"

"And yet, in 1932, when he set the record for both most home runs and highest batting average in a season, he also set another record: most strikeouts. But Babe Ruth isn't remembered for his failures, he's remembered for his successes. Why? Because failure is an event, not an identity. In fact, if you look at the list of record-holders for most strikeouts in MLB history, you'll notice that almost every single one of the top 20 names is also one of the most powerful batters in history, too. And like Babe Ruth, all of them understand something really important: *if you want to hit a lot of home runs, you have to be willing to strike out a lot.*"

Jason nodded, knowing that made sense. Still, it seemed strange. It went against everything he knew and felt about failing. Sensing this, Caroline went on…

"Unfortunately, we've attached so much shame to the event of failure as a culture that most people are simply too afraid of it to ever do what is necessary to become great, and push through however many 'no's' it takes to get to their 'yes,' like Sara Blakely."

"I guess that's right. I just wish I knew how many it takes…"

"Ah, but that's not the point. If you knew the number, you would know the outcome, and the outcome won't help you. Only the process will. It's like that old poem, The Stonecutter's Credo—"

"Pound the stone?!" Caroline nodded, and Jason couldn't believe it. "How do you know that?!"

"Russ told me about it, actually. He said he learned it from a friend of his named T.D." Jason chuckled, as she continued, "Anyway, the poem talks about pounding the stone a hundred times without a single crack showing. So for one hundred blows, the stonecutter appears to be a failure. And if they stopped at blow one hundred, they would stay that way. But instead, blow 101 splits the stone. Now, is the stonecutter any different as a person? Has their identity changed?"

"No," Jason shook his head. "They just swung the hammer one more time."

"Exactly! That swing didn't make them any more or less of a failure than they were on the other hundred swings. What matters is that they kept on swinging."

Jason nodded as she went on, "So whenever you're beginning to doubt yourself, just remember the stonecutter, and remember: <u>life might look like failure 99% of the time</u>. But failure is temporary. And if you choose to always learn and grow from it, then you never really fail at all."

Jason had been so locked into their conversation that when he looked around, he realized the room was mostly empty. He couldn't believe they'd been talking for a few hours. But he was grateful that he'd met Caroline – he felt a lot better now about the job. And for the first time, he actually looked forward to Monday morning: he couldn't wait to put his new knowledge to work.

When Russ finally arrived to drive them home, Jason couldn't help but ask him, "So... why didn't you ever tell me who you were?"

Russ smiled back. "What I do doesn't define who I am, and like I said, there's always more sides to a box."

# CHAPTER 25

# DOOR TO DOOR

JASON WAS AMAZED at how different it felt now that he had shifted his mindset about failure. He felt like he was finally starting to understand the philosophy of pound the stone. Most importantly, he was finally buying into the idea that the most important thing was not hitting his goal, but developing the grit and character he wanted for the rest of his life.

The change in attitude must have been obvious, because multiple people per day were commenting on his infectious passion and energy. Instead of hating the job, Jason actually started to enjoy it. He was so familiar with the books that he was able to connect with each person and ask questions rather than just robotically repeat a pitch. This confidence allowed more of Jason's personality to come through, something he had struggled with all summer.

Still, the results weren't exceptional. He was definitely selling more books than he had before, but it wasn't enough to make up the ground he had failed to cover in the first ten weeks.

And then, it happened.

With just ten days left in the summer, it seemed like a switch flipped. Jason didn't know exactly how it happened, or why. All he knew was that he was suddenly "in the zone" when it came to selling books. It was the same feeling he had when he had an amazing game on the court – one of those games where every pass was on target, and every shot went in.

Each day he managed to sell more and more books. What felt like utter failure just a couple weeks ago was transformed into hope: he was crushing it!

But that hope nose-dived when reality sunk in as he looked at his final numbers. Even with the surge of sales over the past few weeks, he had fallen short by just 23 books.

"It's so much worse this way, knowing I got so close..." Jason said as he and Russ sat out on the porch that night. "I really thought I was going to make it."

"And to think, you were only 1.9 books per week away from playing basketball again." Russ took a sip from a bottle of the *Waiakea* water he loved so much, "It really does come down to inches, doesn't it? The 'little things' really are quite big in the long run. Small things, over time, aren't that small after all."

"Thanks, I heard you the first fifty times you said that this summer..."

"But now you can do more than hear it: you can <u>know</u> it. It reminds me of when a team starts to give up halfway through a game because it starts to look impossible, but then towards the end they catch a little momentum, only to still fall short by two or three points. I always wonder what would have happened if they had just continued to pound the stone without worrying about the scoreboard. It's easy to think it was one big shot, turnover, missed layup, or free throw, that cost them the game, but it is really a whole bunch of little inches added up over the entire game. One play at the beginning of the game, or the middle of the game is just as important as the one with only seconds left on the clock."

Jason knew Russ was right, but it hurt too badly to admit it. Russ excused himself for bed, but Jason wasn't tired. Russ shot him with a knowing glance, "You're hitting the court, aren't you?"

Jason nodded, sad. "Even if I'm not going to make the team, I guess I can always train. It's like T.D. said. Winning or losing, you gotta keep pounding the stone."

Russ smiled. "Jason, even if that's all you've learned from this whole summer, I promise you: it's worth so much more than money, or than making the team."

Jason wanted to believe him, but the words didn't take any sting off the reality.

# CHAPTER 26

## EARLY HOURS

"I'M SORRY, JASON." Coach shook his head, looking down at the sheet of numbers he had received from the bookselling program. "But you knew what you had to do going into this. You had the whole summer to get there, and you didn't."

"But I got so close! It's just a few books, what's the difference?"

"You weren't getting a letter grade on this, Jason. This was pass/fail. You failed. And I'm glad you figured it out eventually, but some opportunities have an expiration date. This one's gone."

Jason pushed back, desperate, "Can I work my way back onto the team somehow? I'm not the same guy I was, trust me." Michael hesitated, and Jason pressed on. "I'll come in an hour early. I'll leave an hour late. I'll put in more time than anyone else on the team, I swear."

Silence fell as Michael processed that. More than anyone, he knew how much Jason hated practice. It had always bothered him. So this was a win-win scenario. But he would still have to get clearance from his A.D. He sighed, "Look, if you start working out at 5 a.m. for two hours before we start, I'll run it past Scott for approval. In the meantime, you will also serve as our team manager."

Jason shot up, smiling. He hated the idea of being the manager, but he was desperate to get back on the team. He shook Michael's hand with gratitude, "Thank you, Coach! Whatever it takes. You won't regret it!"

Michael watched him bounce out of the office. Maybe something did happen over the summer. Jason certainly acted like a different person. And it took some convincing, but Scott was onboard eventually too. They were both curious to see if Jason would actually follow through.

But to Michael's surprise, at 6 a.m. on Monday he found Jason already dripping in sweat doing footwork drills in the gym. Jason gave him a big smile, then went right back to work. Clearly, the kid really wanted this. As Michael watched, the assistant coach came up, surprised.

"Do I need to get my eyes checked? Or is that really the same kid who put his fist through your wall at the end of last year?"

Michael just shrugged. "I guess we'll find out. I told him that if he puts in an extra two hours per day, I might reconsider putting him back on the team. I give him a week before he quits."

"That's generous," the other coach chuckled. "I give him three days."

# CHAPTER 27

# BACK TO SCHOOL

"JASON? EXCUSE ME?"

Jason jerked awake; he had fallen asleep in history class again. The late nights and early mornings were starting to catch up with him. But he knew that second chances don't always come around, so he was determined to make the most of this one.

He apologized to his teacher, as across the room he caught a glimpse of a familiar face: Kaiya. He shot her a tired smile and she smiled back.

After their conversation over the summer, she hadn't responded to any more of his messages. He started to wonder if he was wasting his time trying to get to know her. But that thought disappeared the second he saw her again. She was even more beautiful than he remembered. Her swagger, her smile – she really wasn't like any other girls Jason knew.

She certainly wasn't as easy to hang out with either. He got the sense that she didn't let many people into her world. But he had managed to thaw the ice a little bit by talking with her about some of the other books he'd read over the summer.

After class, she bumped into him playfully. "Hey sleepyhead. You up all night reading again?"

"No way. I'm not a nerd," he said playfully.

"A nerd like me, you mean?" She laughed. He liked that Kaiya didn't take herself that seriously, even though she probably ranked up near the top of their class.

He shook off his sleepiness. "Yeah, I'm just tired. The extra practice sucks. I do three more hours each day, on top of serving as the team manager."

"Isn't that a good thing? I thought that's how you get better."

"Sure, maybe if I knew it would work. But Coach never told me when he would let me know if I can get back on the team again or not."

"So what? Are you looking for an escape hatch out of something you find painful, or do you actually want to get better?"

The way Kaiya said it wasn't judgmental, just direct. Still, Jason snapped back, "I'm not complaining. I just don't like that Coach didn't tell me how long this would go on."

"Well if you don't like how difficult it is, you could always quit."

That just made Jason even angrier. Who did this girl think she was? "Whatever. *You* try doing footwork and conditioning drills for two hours every morning before everyone else, then shooting for an extra hour every night. Then you can talk to me about how difficult anything is."

Kaiya shrugged disarmingly. "Look, *I'm sure it's hard. But hard work is the price of admission for the opportunity to become great at anything, not just basketball. Business, creativity, relationships. Greatness takes resilience. Mastery takes grit.* I thought you understood that. I was finally starting to think you weren't like most people."

With that, she walked off, leaving Jason frustrated. He really liked Kaiya, but he hated everything she had just said. Maybe because it all reminded him of something Russ would say.

On the way to his next class, he got a text from Riley and Aaron, two friends he'd grown up with on the same block. With Jason so focused on basketball, they hung out less now; Riley and Aaron's only 'sport' was partying. Usually anytime they did hang out it involved getting high or buzzed, and today was the same story. They wanted to get high after school, and Jason knew he could really use the release. It sure would feel good to just chill.

But as the last bell rang, Jason knew he had worked too hard to let a moment of emotional pain get in the way of him getting back on the team. He could almost hear T.D. in his head: *"No excuses, pound the stone."* Driven by that thought, he geared up and hit the gym.

But this time, he wasn't alone. Travis was out there already, waiting for him. "Need one more?"

Jason smiled, grateful for at least one friend who would join him in his "pound the stone" workout. They went right to work, taking game shots at game speed, and trying to master their footwork. And as one hour melted into two, it felt just like that night during the summer. Jason was grateful for a friend like Travis.

# CHAPTER 28

# LOSING SEASON

As JASON CONTINUED putting in his early and late hours, the season began, and the start was rocky. The team had lost two All State seniors and struggled from day one, losing five straight games.

Coach Michael seemed to be going out of his mind trying to figure out how to motivate the team, because not much was working. No matter how much he yelled, no matter how many extra rounds of conditioning they ran after each loss as punishment, nothing seemed to work.

As hard as it was for the team, it was even more frustrating for Jason to watch from the sidelines. Knowing he could help but not being allowed to felt unfair and cruel, but he used his anger as motivation instead. Every set of sprints he ran, every shot he took, every morning he woke up tired to the bone, he thought about the fact that his own team was losing, and he wasn't on it.

He needed the motivation, too. Even his summer selling books didn't compare to how tired he was now. But he kept on pounding the stone, knowing it had to pay off eventually.

Travis began joining his morning workouts as well. Jason knew that as a senior and a captain, Travis was probably feeling a lot of heat from Coach. Coach expected a lot from the leaders on the team, and often blamed them if and when anything went wrong. But if Travis was feeling pressured, he did a good job of hiding it. Instead, he just kept encouraging Jason.

Jason thanked him as they finished a set of sprints. "I just keep telling myself that I can practice longer than Coach can keep holding out from letting me back on the team."

Travis laughed. "If things keep going the way they are, you're probably right."

And he was. A week later, four weeks after Jason had started his extra hours of training, Coach called him into his office. He handed Jason his jersey back, and simply said, "Let's go to work."

Later, Jason found out that it wasn't just his extra time pounding the stone that convinced Coach. It was Travis. He had eventually gone to Michael directly and vouched for Jason, asked him to bring Jason back, telling him that the team needed him and that he had seen first hand the transformation taking place in his life over the summer.

Jason was overcome with gratitude, but when he brought it up to thank Travis, he just smiled. "No need to thank me. You're the one who put in the work. Now let's go win some games!"

# CHAPTER 29

## "TRAVIS..."

AND WIN SOME games they did. The rest of the season flew past, as Jason jumped right back in to the mix. While he had had his doubts about the training he'd been putting in, he quickly saw how it affected his play. He was faster and stronger than last season, and his endurance had improved as well. However, it took him a while to catch up to the new schemes Coach was running that season. So each night he spent an hour in the film room, studying tape.

Within a few weeks, things started to click, and Jason felt the thrill of competing in a game kick back in as he and the team began to win. First one game, then another, then a whole hot streak of six in a row. Soon, they were on a path right back to where they'd been last year – the State Finals. First, they had to get through semis, and Jason knew what that meant.

He'd be playing against Hudson High and Trey, the guard he got in a fight with last year. Something about the guy just rubbed Jason the wrong way. He was a brash, cocky player, but he was also really good. He played relentless, in-your-face defense and loved to push the boundaries – the same as Jason did.

This time around, he did his best to control his emotions, and focus on the basics. He knew that this was a huge game. If they didn't win, they were out of the semis. This game was their season.

And at first, it was going well. Jason and the rest of the Raiders were in sync, running the system to a "T" and working well as a single unit. But by the third quarter, Hudson had their number. Jason found himself eating elbows from Trey on every drive to the hoop. He did his best to keep his cool, but as he ducked in and jumped for a layup – WHAM! Trey blindsided him, throwing a hip-check into Jason that sent him crashing to the court.

The whistle shrieked, and as Jason picked himself up, wincing, he felt the familiar rush of anger.

"Chill, chill, chill!" Travis pulled Jason to his feet, calming him. "Just hit the free throws. You know he is just trying to rattle you."

Jason took a deep breath as he got to the line. He did everything he could to shut out the blast of rage in his thoughts, but it was too much. He missed both free throws. He cursed, now he was just as angry with himself as he was with Trey. The whistle blew again, and he saw Coach waving him over. He jogged to the bench, and before he could say anything --

"Jason, you're out. That guy's in your head. I'm not letting you lose this like you did last year."

Nothing Jason said would change his mind. So he just walked to the far end of the bench and threw a towel over his head, sulking. He couldn't believe it. After all the time he put in over the summer, he blew it on something this stupid. He watched helplessly as the game's energy shifted away from the Raiders, and their opponents ran away with it, winning by fourteen.

Coach was so angry he threw a chair into the locker room wall afterward.

This time his fury landed on Travis, who didn't even have a bad game. But as one of the seniors, he was held to a higher standard. As they got back on the bus, Jason noticed Travis was quiet. That was rare for him;

usually he was that kid who always had a smile. Jason asked if he was okay, and he just shrugged. "You win some. You lose some... I guess."

The next week at school Travis seemed back to his normal energetic self. He even found Jason in the hall and gave him a gift – an iTunes gift card.

Jason thanked him, but Travis shrugged it off. "No, thank YOU! I'm glad you made it back on the team, I think that's the only reason we even got as far as we did."

Jason thanked him again and didn't really think much of it.

After third period the next day, he noticed a group of police squad cars and an ambulance clustered around the entrance to the basketball stadium. A crowd of students were standing there watching something. They were quiet, speaking in whispers. Clearly something was wrong.

Jason saw someone familiar in the crowd. "Kaiya?! Hey!" She turned toward him and her face was frozen in shock. "What's going on? Did something happen?"

She nodded, horrified. "You didn't hear? He jumped from the roof... he killed himself."

"Who?"

Her voice shook as she answered. "Travis."

# CHAPTER 30

# AN ANCHOR FOR YOUR SOUL

JASON HAD NEVER seen so many people wearing black.

The school gym was packed, a standing-room-only crowd gathered for Travis's funeral. His family sat in the front row. They looked like zombies.

Jason sat with the team, all of them stone-cold and quiet. They didn't look at each other. No one knew what to say. What <u>could</u> you say? Travis was one of them, one of their brothers. He was a constant source of energy and life to the team, who did nothing but give to everyone around him. He had well above a 4.0 GPA, captain of the basketball team, and he was the class President. How could someone like that, do something like this? It just didn't make sense.

Jason had found out that the day before he killed himself, Travis had gone around to other teammates and given them gifts as well. He had also stopped into classes of old teachers to thank them. It was like his "goodbye tour" before leaving the world. But to anyone who knew him, that was just Travis being himself. That's the kind of guy he was.

Since the moment Kaiya told him what happened, Jason's world had turned upside down. Never in a million years did he suspect that someone like Travis would do this. Travis was a guy who seemed to have it all in life. Why would he want to end it?!

No answer that Jason could think of or had heard from other people made any sense at all. Apparently Travis was rejected by his top two colleges, and the team's loss was another big failure on top of that. But honestly, basketball was only a game. And Travis would clearly go to a good college, even if it wasn't the exact one he wanted. Jason couldn't make sense of it.

As the procession ended, a guy in a suit stepped forward. He introduced himself as Judah Smith.

He looked young for a pastor, with a boyish face framed by glasses. But when he spoke, the authority in his voice removed any doubt about his wisdom. Jason was hooked immediately.

Judah paced, mic in hand. "My father was my hero. He was larger than life, and when he passed away from cancer in my early thirties, it was the hardest thing I had ever been through. It felt like I was drowning. I know that is how many of you are feeling today. Maybe all you want in this moment is some way to escape it. To climb into a helicopter and fly up and out of the storm. But that's not actually what God promises us in moments like this."

Jason leaned forward, curious. He'd never heard someone talk about God like this.

"In moments like this, God doesn't promise us a helicopter. He promises us an anchor for our soul. I never really understood what that meant until I lost my dad. The funny thing about an anchor is that it actually keeps you stationed in the same place, and it keeps you secure, no matter what kind of storm you're in the middle of.

And I know that's not always what we want to hear. It certainly wasn't what I wanted to hear when I lost my father. I wanted to run from the pain, not stay in it and feel it. But the thing I learned about pain from that time in my life, is that pain can be extremely valuable. It can teach us things we would never otherwise know.

Look, we are all in this together, and my encouragement for all of us is to be kind, empathetic, and loving, because every person we meet is fighting raging storms we often know nothing about. I know this tragedy doesn't make sense to many of you, and it sure doesn't to me. But this I do know for sure; God loved Travis with a reckless and unconditional love, just like he does you and me. Would you bow your heads with me?"

Jason wasn't usually one for praying, but he bowed his head as Judah prayed...

"Jesus, I pray that your peace would fill our hurting and broken hearts. I pray that you would wrap us in your arms and comfort us with your love. We thank you that even when we go through unfathomable storms, we still have an anchor for our soul in you."

# CHAPTER 31

## MOVING ON

FOR THE NEXT few weeks, Jason couldn't shake Judah's words. They echoed in his mind wherever he went. When they did, it just made him think about Travis even more. That just made him uncomfortable, because he didn't really know what to say. Maybe there just wasn't anything to say at all.

It didn't help that the whole school seemed to be stuck in the same place. People didn't know how to look at each other, or talk to each other. They mostly seemed to have the same weird surface conversations, like a song on repeat. "So weird, right?" "Yeah... he was so young..."

Jason had never realized what a difference one person could make in his life, but now that Travis was gone, every day was filled with reminders. They always walked from one side of school to another between classes, and he had gotten used to 'talking shop' about the day's practice, and their upcoming games. The first day Travis wasn't there, Jason walked outside to avoid their route, despite the cold.

It was so weird. He could still hear Travis's voice, telling a joke or asking him about his day. The fact that he would never speak to him again took his breath away with the harshest pain he'd ever felt. He did his best to just not think about it, put on a strong face, and move on. The last thing the school needed was another hurting kid walking around. He just wanted to get back to normal.

He wasn't alone, either. When the school brought a grief counselor in for a special session for the team to help them 'process' Travis's death, no one spoke more than a few words. No one looked at each other. Just like Jason, they were sad Travis was gone, but they all seemed ready to move on.

But on the walk home after practice, Jason couldn't stop thinking about it. No matter how hard he tried, the pain came back, which just made him angrier. He didn't want to feel anything right now. As he got home, he saw a familiar car waiting for him: that boxy Subaru he hated so much.

Russ didn't need to say anything; Jason could tell by his eyes that he knew what had happened. So all he said was, "Let's get some food."

In the car, he didn't say a word. They just drove. When they got to the restaurant, Russ ordered for them, and as they waited for the food he looked at Jason. Like, <u>really looked</u> at him.

"I'm so sorry to hear about your friend, Jason." It was said with a depth of care, sincerity, and warmth Jason had never experienced from another man.

Jason didn't really know what to say. "I mean, yeah... Travis was... he..."

Jason's vision got cloudy and he felt tears sting his eyes. The mask he had fought to keep in place was slipping, and he couldn't stop it any more. He sniffed at his running nose and turned away. But Russ was already there, wrapping him in a hug.

"You don't need to say anything. I'm with you." He kept repeating "I'm with you" as a big sob shook Jason. He had never gotten a hug from an adult other than his mom, so he didn't know what to do but cry.

Suddenly everything he'd been holding up inside of him released, and for the first time in a week he could think clearly again.

He thought he wanted to hear wise words from Russ, something that would ease the pain, but he realized that sometimes, the most beneficial thing in a moment like that was to simply hear and feel; the only thing Russ did say: "I am with you."

# CHAPTER 32

## BRING YOUR BASKETBALL

THE WEEKS AFTER blurred past. Even though life went back to normal, something was missing. It still felt like a hole had been shot through the middle of his life. His time with Russ helped, and he kept busy with school and keeping up his training for basketball. But every time he walked onto the court, he would remember Travis. It hurt not to see him there.

Eventually, Jason began to practice in the gym less. Instead, he ran stairs at the football field or practiced on the outside courts. Anytime anyone asked how he was doing, he just smiled and told them everything was cool. It was just easier that way.

One day he was walking with Kaiya to class when she asked that same question. He gave his usual response, but she shook her head. "Jason, I know guys like to be strong and silent, but I don't believe for a second that you're okay after a friend as good as Travis has passed away. How are you doing, really? How's your heart?"

He knew that Kaiya saw straight through him. But still, he couldn't admit what was really going on to her. It was just too hard. He stuttered, trying to find the right words, but Kaiya just shook her head. "If you can't talk about it, that's fine. What are you doing tomorrow after school?"

Jason shrugged, "Practicing, probably."

"Cool. If you want, I'd like to take you to meet a friend of mine. We can go after school."

Jason nodded, "Sure." He didn't really feel like it, but he wanted to spend time with Kaiya. She'd been a good friend to him through this, and had consistently checked in on him. In a strange way, he felt closer to her in spite of how hard everything around him was.

As they parted ways, she stopped, adding, "Oh, and bring your basketball!"

Jason couldn't figure out who this friend could possibly be, but he was curious to find out. So the next day, he showed up outside school with a basketball, ready for anything.

# CHAPTER 33

# LAYERS AND LIGHT

KAIYA PULLED INTO a parking lot, smiling at Jason. "We're here. Come on!"

They were at a community park. As they walked over to the basketball courts, he saw a little kid shooting free throws. Well, trying to shoot free throws. The best shot bounced off the rim, but this guy kept enthusiastically chasing his ball down, getting back to the line, and trying again.

There was something awkward about his form, and as they got closer, Jason realized why. Kaiya walked right up to him. "Ryan!" He saw her and gave a shout of joy as the world's biggest smile spread across his face. He practically jumped on her as he gave her a bear hug and she spun him around. The Down syndrome stunted his growth, so even though he was ten years old, he was the size of an average six-year-old. He laughed with infectious joy as she put him down.

Without missing a beat, he marched over to Jason with the same smile and reached out to hug him. It was an awkward hug for Jason as Ryan was really just hugging the leg of his 6'4" frame. "Hi!" Said Ryan with his own unique dialect that came from a somewhat uncooperative tongue.

"Ryan, this is my friend Jason. Jason, this is my friend Ryan. Jason is the basketball player I was telling you about. He is really good!"

Jason blushed. He didn't even know Kaiya had ever watched him play a game. Ryan jumped up and down with excitement, "Would you like to shoot some hoops with him?"

Ryan squealed and turned to shoot an air ball that wasn't even close, but with the joy on his face you would have thought he had hit a game winner in triple overtime of the NBA Finals.

They shot for about an hour, and Ryan loved it. He especially loved when Jason would dunk. He got an even bigger kick out of when Jason went to tomahawk one and it clanged off the back of the rim not landing until soaring past half court. Ryan fell over on the ground he was laughing so hard.

Jason looked over at Kaiya to see pure joy on her face as she watched them. She locked eyes with Jason, and for a moment they shared a connection that was definitely more than "friends."

Ryan laughed and laughed with pure happiness, like he had just opened a Christmas present. He begged Jason to dunk again – and again – and again. And each time, he celebrated with the same incredible joy. Jason was amazed by it. No matter what they did, Ryan's love for it, and the joy on his face, never once changed.

Finally, Jason took a breather on the bleachers with Kaiya. They watched Ryan play, chasing the ball everywhere excitedly. Every single shot he took missed, but he never once complained. He just seemed happy just to be there.

Kaiya stirred, "I love Ryan. He's literally one of my favorite humans. Such a cool kid."

"Yeah. He's just... he's so different from anyone I've ever met. Why do you think that is?"

"He lives entirely in the moment." Emotion welled up in Kaiya's eyes. "Knowing him reminds me to do the same. Not many people know this, but I lost my baby brother when I was nine. And what I learned is that, losing someone can make you not love anyone out of the fear of losing people, or it can teach you to value and treasure every single moment you have with people."

Jason nodded, as she continued, "When we get hurt, we often try and cover up the pain. It's the natural reaction, but that usually doesn't help it get better. Think of when you get hit somewhere, what do you do? You immediately grab it to try and create a layer of protection. And as you get older you layer protection, over protection, over protection. Eventually, you cover up the light inside of you that is meant to shine brightly. You see that light in little children all the time, but it is rare to find an adult with their light still shining. It's not that the light has been put out. The light still exists inside all of us, but for most people it is hidden beneath layers of pain and attempted self-protection, which often becomes self-sabotage."

Jason just listened, blown away by Kaiya's maturity and understanding. "In order to experience the joy of a child, we have to be willing to open ourselves up again and let our light shine bright. *When we shine the way we are intended to, not with arrogance, but with authentic joy, peace, wholeness, and contentment, we allow others to slowly peel back their layers and shine as well."*

Jason tried to process that, blown away. "Um, that was some... wow. How did you learn that?"

"From watching Ryan. You know what they say, 'actions speak louder than words.'"

"Yeah, they do." Jason smiled, and Kaiya smiled back. There it was again, that electric connection. But as the moment stretched, Ryan rushed over toward them...

"Bed tiiiime!!" he shouted, like he was even excited for that.

"We gotta get him home, it's past his bed time." Kaiya said with a smile.

# CHAPTER 34

# THE PATH TO MASTERY

THE END OF the school year approached, and Jason knew he had to figure out his summer plans.

A few of the other guys on the team were playing AAU ball, and he knew the potential for exposure to college scouts, and thus college scholarships, that came with playing in that league. He could get his name out there, show what he could do, and play against and with a lot of the best high school players in the state.

But still, something stopped him. He knew that he still had unfinished business elsewhere, and he couldn't shake the feeling that he needed to finish what he'd started. He worked really hard last summer to find the groove during the last few weeks, and he didn't want to waste that. This time, he'd show that not only could he hit that 1,200-book sales goal -- he could <u>double</u> it.

Unlike last year, he was actually excited to go through the training this time. Instead of T.D. though, the keynote speaker was a guy named Rory Vaden. He wore a suit and tie, and spoke with the precision of a master storyteller.

"I run my own business, and each year we hire new salespeople. And I'll tell you right now that if you showed up in my office with a resume that listed four years in this program, and you were up for the job against someone with a resume that listed four years at Harvard, Duke, or Yale, I would hire you over that person in a heartbeat.

Why? Because I know from experience that college simply doesn't provide the level of grit, character and perseverance that going through this program does. That's right, not so long ago I sat where you're sitting. And for five summers, I sold books door to door just like you. Now our consulting business I cofounded does over eight figures in revenue per year, and I can trace a line from my summers selling books to where I am now. Do you want to know what that line looks like? Here it is...

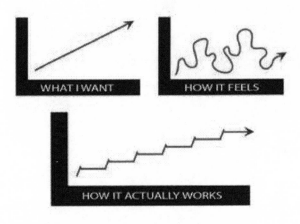

The path to mastery is a lot of things, but most of all, it's not a straight line.

You know the other surprising thing about mastery? While mastery itself is an incredible thing, getting there isn't actually that exciting. Excellence is mundane.[12] There is nothing flashy about doing the hard work in the dark while the rest of the world is asleep. There's nothing sexy about putting in twelve to fourteen hour days trying and failing to master your craft. And the final thing that most people fail to understand, but that I have found most crucial to my success in business and relationships:"

12   Read the article, *The Mundanity of Excellence*, by Daniel F. Chambliss

Jason looked up at the screen as Rory shared the quote.

**_Find your uniqueness and exploit it in the service of others._**

As Rory finished, Jason realized just how applicable those same principles were to basketball. It was like T.D. had said just a year ago: a 'pound the stone' mentality applies to everything in life.

After training, he was happy to knock on a familiar front door again. Russ and Jan welcomed him back in like a son, and it felt great to be around them again. He was also just happy to be away from his school, and all the reminders of the tough year he had just been through.

But if he thought this summer would be any easier, he was dead wrong.

# CHAPTER 35

# DAVID BEFORE GOLIATH

THE FIRST DAY of sales was a total blowout. Jason felt awkward, stumbling over his words and messing up what might have been sure sales last summer. By the time he made it back for dinner, he was so frustrated he barely said a word. As soon as he finished helping Jan with the dishes, he grabbed his gear and headed out to his old practice court.

He was looking forward to a night on the court alone, but as he got there he saw someone else was already there practicing: T.D. himself.

Jason was shocked, as the big man stopped shooting to give him a fist bump. "Hi Jason. Russell said you might need a little help this summer. I'm really sorry to hear about your friend."

"Yeah, it's okay. Thanks."

"So, how did the season go?"

"It was fine, I guess. That practice you gave helped."

"Did it?" T.D. smiled, "So you really followed through on the workout I gave you?"

Jason stumbled, "Well, yeah, I mean... actually..."

"In case you forgot, maybe this will help." From his pocket, T.D. handed Jason the <u>very same workout he gave him a year ago</u>, crumpled just like it was when Jason threw it away.

"You found it?" Jason flushed with embarrassment. "I'm sorry, it's just... I didn't think it would work. I've wanted to ask you all year, where is the rest of it?"

"The rest of it? There isn't any."

"What do you mean? Those six basic drills, that's it?!" T.D. nodded, as Jason tried to wrap his mind around it. "You've gotta be kidding me... you don't do anything else for practice?"

"Is there something wrong with that?"

"No, it's just... I thought it would be more complicated than some basic drills."

"Jason, greatness is simple. Nothing complicated about it. Have you ever watched us play?" T.D. said with a chuckle. "And if a player can't master the basics, they'll never master anything bigger. The foundation of every win in my career isn't any elaborate play scheme or coaching strategy, though I've benefitted from those. It's what's on that sheet. Without that, and the tens of thousands of hours I've spent mastering the skills from those drills, you wouldn't even know my name."

That landed hard with Jason as he nodded. T.D. sensed his hesitation. "Let me ask you, Jason, have you ever heard of David and Goliath?"

"You serious? Yeah, of course. Everyone has."

"So, you know how that story ends, right?" Jason nodded, of course. "But have you thought about how it begins? It begins with David being overlooked and underestimated his entire life. We blow David up into this mythological character, but long before Goliath, his job was taking care of the sheep. It was a degrading, humiliating job, but he did it faithfully. Day in and day out, in heat and cold and rain and mud, he took care of those sheep. Every day, for years.

Now, in life everyone will face a 'Goliath' moment. And in that moment most people think, 'if I knew this moment was coming I would have prepared better. If I had known I would be here, I would have been so much more faithful in all the little, seemingly insignificant details.'"

Jason nodded as T.D. went on, "*The cool thing that happens when we become faithful to the process, to the little things, to the 'sheep-tending' seasons in our lives, is that it's actually building and refining our character so that when those Goliath opportunities come, we can step up with the conviction that only comes from incredible preparation.*

That's what I want for you. It's cool, the basketball stuff, but this is about more than that. Your Goliath moments can come on or off the court. When they do, your fate won't be determined by what you do in that moment. Instead, your fate was already determined a long time ago, based off of your willingness, or unwillingness, to suffer, sacrifice, and be incredibly faithful with the little 'sheep' in your life that feel insignificant at the time.

I can promise you something, Jason: *if you truly fall in love with the process, you will eventually love what the process produces.* 'Eventually' is the key word. Everyone's 'eventually' is different, and we can't control when it arrives. All we can control is our faithfulness to tending sheep. Your 'eventually' might come tomorrow or 25 years from now, but I promise that if you will fall in love with the process, you will eventually love what the process produces. Victory in your Goliath moments starts long before, when you faithfully tend sheep like David did."

# CHAPTER 36

# BLAME VS. RESPONSIBILITY

JASON WAS ENCOURAGED by T.D.'s wisdom. He did his best to remind himself of David spending those early years being extraordinarily faithful to very ordinary things. *He reminded himself that greatness takes time, and that the price of admission to greatness is dirty hard work.*

But that wore off as the first weeks of summer passed. Some days it felt like he hadn't ever sold a book before, and the "in the zone" feeling from last summer seemed like some distant memory. Jason started to question choosing to spend his summer selling books again in the first place.

One night as he was helping Jan clean the dishes, she asked him what was happening.

He couldn't hold back the frustration, "Nothing is working! I'm doing everything I can. I'm following all of Russ's secrets to success, and every morning I remember what T.D. told me about being extraordinarily faithful to ordinary things. But what good is it if I do all that stuff and people still won't listen to me or buy from me or take me seriously?"

Despite his anger, Jan stayed calm. "Tell me, Jason. Where is this coming from?"

"I don't know, it's fine. I'll get over it. Life's just not fair, that's all."

"Oh? How is life not fair?"

Jason looked at her like she grew another head. "It just isn't—not for guys like me. I didn't have a dad growing up, I didn't have money; I had zero advantages. Some people get handed everything, other people don't. I don't have parents who buy me the best gear, or pay for me to play in a summer league or pay for one-on-one coaching. I know that the deck is stacked against me. I know it won't be as easy for me as it is for everyone else."

"You do, really?" There was a twinkle in Jan's eye. Obviously she was holding something back.

"What? You think I don't?"

"Jason, it's true that we all start from different places in life. But if someone is truly great, there's a reason things seem easy for them. The easier they make it look, the more work they've put in in the dark. Do you know who else had no father and no money growing up? Steve Jobs. He was the illegitimate child of immigrants. He was adopted. He grew up in a house that's smaller than this one, in a neighborhood much poorer than most. He was forced to change schools at age 11 because of how relentlessly he was bullied in school. After dropping out of college, he had to recycle bottles in order to have enough money to eat. Now, how 'easy' do you think he had it going from there to the man he became?"

"Probably not very easy." Jason was stunned. He had never heard that before.

"When you pull back the layers on the people who have lived extraordinary lives you rarely find a silver spoon or childhood prodigy. Occasionally, you do, but more often than not you find people who decided to do the very best they could, with what they had, right where they were at.

*Life is about 10% what you have when you begin, things like natural talent and opportunity, and 90% what you do with it.*

Maybe this is why more often than not, those who start with less accomplish so much more. I know that Russ and I wouldn't be anywhere near where we are if we could have gotten a comfortable job out of college. We wouldn't have ever truly learned how to hustle for real had we not been turned down for entry-level jobs everywhere we looked. *We were forced to cut our teeth in the street, and that experience paid off exponentially over time.*

Our culture is obsessed with eliminating struggle. There are parents whose goal is that their kids want for nothing. But what if they're handicapping them instead? Our fear of failure for the next generation is creating people primed for mediocrity at best and crippled at worst, in comparison to their potential. *Experiencing repeated failure and lack of resources forces you to develop deep levels of grit, intellectual creativity, and resourcefulness others have never tapped into.*

But reaching your greatest potential depends on whether you lean into that process, or run from it. Most people choose to run. They would rather fixate on the 10% of their lives they can't control, and so they complain and blame everyone and everything. But *the funny thing about blame is that while it might temporarily make us feel better, it does absolutely nothing to create a better tomorrow. Anyone can blame, but very few have the courage to take responsibility.*

Are there systemic issues in this country? Absolutely.
Is life much more challenging for different groups of people? Absolutely.
Do some people have it harder than others? Absolutely.

Blame is about the past, though. Responsibility is about making the most of the present to create a better future.

Everyone wants things to change, but nobody wants *to* change. Everybody wants things to get better, but very few are willing to become the change they wish to see happen in their world.

It's easy to blame, it's hard to take responsibility.

It's so easy to look at someone else and say… 'Oh if I had their athleticism, I would be a millionaire… If I had her voice, I would have a record deal… If I came from that family, I would be killing it in business… If I had their budget, talent, good looks, height… then everything would be different.' But that's a lie.

The hard truth is that every person has two or three ideas or natural abilities that would make them a millionaire if they would work hard enough to see them all the way through. But the reality is, most people quit when things get uncomfortable. Forget the fact that you must persevere through hard, painful, exhausted, and on the cusp of total disaster to make it to that level. Everyone has the potential, but few will develop the grit.

*The most valuable things in life you can't be given, and they can't be bought. No amount of money, family status, or talent can buy character and grit… they can only be earned.* And Jason, I know that's what you're doing. You're earning them right now. So stay patient and consistent. It will all come together in time."

Jason felt like he'd just taken a big drink from a firehose of wisdom. He thought about it that night as he hit the court for practice, hoping that Jan was right.

# CHAPTER 37

# SLEEP THROUGH THE STORMS

THE RUST SLOWLY came off, and Jason fell into a rhythm. Sales came easier, and while it wasn't the crazy numbers that happened at the end of last summer, he was making good progress.

The heat and long hours were made easier by the fact that he also really looked forward to his training each night. He felt like he was finally starting to get everything T.D. had been teaching him. But that's not the only thing he was excited about. He knew that he and Kaiya were "just friends" but it felt like their connection was growing stronger even with distance between them. They didn't talk every day, but when they did it was always the bright spot of Jason's day.

Which is why what happened next totally blindsided him.

He was taking his lunch break one day in a park, eating the sandwich that Jan had packed for him. He was flipping through his Instagram feed when he saw it...

A picture of Kaiya, smiling, with her arm around another guy. But it wasn't just any guy: it was Trey, the guard who played for Hudson. *The same guy Jason punched in the face: his nemesis.*

Pain hit Jason in the stomach and he felt a blast of angry blood rushing to his head. He couldn't believe it. This felt like nothing he had ever felt before – betrayal, but more personal somehow. Didn't Kaiya know how much he hated this guy? Was she doing this on purpose somehow to mess with him? It felt like a sick joke that he couldn't figure out the punch line to.

He walked around in a daze the rest of the day. When he got home, he went straight to his room after dinner and locked the door. He didn't want to talk to or see anyone.

He tried to shake it off the next day and just get back to work, but it didn't really work. He went back to Russ and Jan's, changed, and hit the basketball court. Maybe a workout would help get him out of it. But that just made it worse. With every shot and every drill he thought about Trey. And thinking of a guy like that getting the chance to be with a girl as great as Kaiya spun Jason's head in circles. It made him a weird combination of angry and sad.

He went home even more depressed than before, a haze hanging over him. At home, Russ was out on the porch as usual, reading a book.

"You look like a guy who's ready to punch a hole in a wall again." Jason just nodded and sat in one of the porch chairs. "What's going on, son?"

As Jason told him, he didn't expect Russ to get it. But instead, Russ nodded and got silent. "I'm sorry you're going through that. That's one of the most frustrating things I can imagine as a guy your age. I know this because it happened to me."

"Really?"

"Sure did. I met Jan in college, but she wouldn't give me the time of day. I had to wait, just like you. So we became friends, but then she started dating this no-good punk named Cory, who I hated. But I had to watch the girl I was in love with go for him instead of me. It was brutal."

"What happened?"

A big smile broke over Russ's face. "Well, obviously I got the girl. That's a story for another time, though. Tonight, I want to tell you a different story. It's a story about a ship."

"A ship?"

"Yes. A group of men were putting together a sailing crew for a dangerous, epic journey, and they wanted the best sailors in the world. One man stood out from the rest. He told them that he had plenty of experience to qualify for the job, but the only thing they needed to know is that 'I sleep through the storms.' They were confused, but he just repeated, that he always did his job so well that he could sleep through any storm. They hired him on the spot."

Russ smiled, getting into the story. "During the first week of the trip they encountered a ferocious storm in the Pacific Ocean, one of the worst hurricanes of all time. Waves as high as mountain ranges. Sure enough, this sailor was sleeping. They tried to wake him up, but he told them to leave him alone: he sleeps through the storms. The next morning when things had settled down, they realized that every single tiny thing that this man was responsible for on the boat was still secured. Every single knot was still tied tight. Everyone was in awe."

"Yeah, I would be too! Guy was good at his job."

Russ nodded, "Jason, the storms in life are inevitable. It doesn't matter if you are a 'good' person or a 'bad' person, the storms will come. My hope is that you will start doing all the things necessary to prepare for when the next storm comes. Because they always come, just like the seasons. When it comes to relationships, love is an action, not a feeling. Kaiya's choice is somewhat irrelevant if you love her. If you really love someone then their behavior is somewhat irrelevant. It shouldn't determine your behavior, or that is just manipulation on your part, not love. A very wise man once said, 'love is patient, love is kind, love bears all things, endures all things, love never ends.'[13] Feelings come and go, but love endures forever."

Jason nodded, encouraged by this strange story of the sailor who slept through storms.

"One other thing, Jason, while we're talking about storms," Russ continued. "They can often come when you least expect them. For me, that was in my mid-30's, after some massive successes in my career. On the outside, it looked like everything was going so well. It looked like I was living my dream. But inside, I was lost in a hurricane of darkness. I spent every moment of that time deathly afraid of failure. Eventually, I found myself literally standing on the edge of a bridge one night, wondering if maybe the world might be better off without me.'"

"Really? You?!" Jason couldn't believe it. Russ was probably the strongest person he'd ever met. But the older man nodded, tears in his eyes. Shaken by the memory.

"I was so afraid of appearing weak by reaching out and just talking to someone about my fear, that I almost ended my life." Russ breathed deep, "Jason, this is why chasing outcomes is so dangerous. It can literally cost you your life. Michael Phelps went through something similar, even after he had already won 18 gold medals. When the storms come, what matters is who you've become in the process of your life. Because if you've been faithful in the little things, in every area of your life, and put your trust in the right place, then when the storms come, you'll be able to sleep through them."

---

13 The wise man is Paul, from 1 Corinthians 13

# CHAPTER 38

# CAN'T CHEAT THE PERSON IN THE MIRROR

Russ had helped ease Jason's mind, but he still had trouble keeping his optimism up.

Any time he stopped to think about Trey being with Kaiya, it seemed to derail his mood. The rhythm he had enjoyed in sales for the past few weeks fell off entirely. That piled frustration on top of his already-bad mood, and it became a vicious cycle of negativity.

He began to second-guess his choice about how he was spending the summer, and found himself scrolling through the social media feeds of some of his teammates, watching as they played through their AAU schedule traveling around the state. The broken-down asphalt court that he visited every night to pound the stone alone started looking worse and worse in comparison.

Even his customers seemed colder, ruder, and more impatient. He could read their reactions the moment they decided not to buy a book, and that moment was happening faster and faster. Each day was a new battle, and Jason didn't have to look at his numbers to know that he was behind.

After dinner one night, he was helping Jan clean up the dishes. "I'm trying not to put blame where it doesn't belong, but honestly, it's so hard selling to people who are so rude and so selfish that sometimes they don't even let me talk!"

Jan nodded, understanding. Then, she asked him, "Jason, remember what I asked you a year ago? I asked you if you would buy a book from you right now."

"Yeah, I remember that."

Jan pointed to the mirror hanging above the sink. "Well, take a look. Would you?"

Jason felt dumb for doing it, but he cleaned off his hands and walked over to the mirror. He looked himself in the eye. At first, he noticed nothing different. "Yeah, I guess I would."

"Are you sure? Sell yourself a book right now, without speaking."

Jason felt even sillier, but he did as she asked, acting like he was selling a book to someone on the other side of the mirror. As he did, he noticed something: the guy in the mirror looking back at him looked angry. He stopped and adjusted, trying to put on a charming smile. But still, there was something really off about it: he was clearly faking it.

"Now, answer it again: would you buy a book from you right now?"

Jason's fake smile disappeared as he admitted, "No, ma'am."

"Have you ever heard of mirror neurons, Jason?" He shook his head. "Mirror neurons are our brain's mechanism for creating empathy. They fire when we see something we recognize in another person. If we see someone else stub their toe or hit their head on something, we wince or cringe, because our mirror neurons recognize that same feeling from our own experience.

This intricate and amazing system in our brains explains something that I've found fascinating. The fact is, we tend to see in other people what we most dislike in ourselves. And no one likes seeing their own problems staring them in the face like that.

*The hard truth is that so often, what we see in others says a lot more about us than it does about them.* So when you knock on someone's door and try to sell them a book, what you're seeing in them isn't their rudeness or coldness or impatience: Jason, it's yours. We project our fears, insecurities, and anger onto them.

You've heard the phrase, "the ball don't lie," right?" She said.

'Yes Jan." He responded with more than a little annoyance.

"Hey, I just wanted to check! Anyway, it has nothing to do with the ball. The ball doesn't have a conscious or subconscious mind. In any given second your brain is processing 11 million bits of information, but your conscious mind is only aware of around 40 of those bits. Meaning you and I are unaware of around 99.9999% of what our brain is processing. A fancy way of explaining that it is virtually impossible to cheat the person in the mirror.

When you go to the line but you know you didn't get fouled, you are more likely to miss the free throw because your subconscious—and sometimes your conscious mind—knows you didn't deserve to be there.

*You can cheat a lot of people in this life, but you can never cheat the person in the mirror.*

Look, I'm not your coach, but maybe you should take tonight off of physical training and do some mental training." Jan said with a smile. "Watch the movie CREED. The whole movie is about a young man just like you who realizes that his greatest obstacle is not Trey, the government, his skin color, or anyone else. His greatest opponent is the man in the mirror."

Jason wouldn't take a night off training for many people, but there was something about the intensity and care in Jan's voice that made him decide to take her suggestion.

As he lay in bed that night watching the film, it began to sink in: he really was his biggest enemy. *It wasn't him versus the world, it was him versus himself.* And then an even bigger gut-punch realization landed. The reason Trey frustrated him so much actually had nothing to do with Trey – it had to do with himself. Every time he looked at Trey, it was a mirror reflecting back to Jason areas in his own life he would rather not deal with.

It was a sobering thought. Jason knew he had some work to do.

CHAPTER 39

# CIRCUMSTANCE AND BEING

THE NEXT NIGHT when Jason got home, Russ wasn't alone on the porch like usual. He was joined by a big gregarious guy who introduced himself as Augie, an old friend of Russ's.

"So, are you a street-sweeper too?" Jason couldn't resist the dig.

Augie boomed out a laugh. "Worse. I'm a monk! Well, a wannabe monk, anyway. I often work with the Trappist monks of Mepkin Abbey. In another life I was a CEO just like Russ."

"Got it. So what are the street sweeper and the 'wannabe monk' talking about? I'm curious!"

Russ and Augie exchanged glances, as Jason sat down. Russ began, "Well, Augie was telling me a really sad statistic. Around 60% of NBA players go broke within 5 years of retirement."

"What?! Really?" Jason was shocked. He'd always imagined that the massive amounts of money you could make as a pro would be far more than enough to pay your bills for life.

"Really. It's unfortunate, but that is what happens when someone confuses a transformation of circumstance with a transformation of being."

128

Augie noticed the confusion on Jason's face and chuckled, "Here, let me break it down for you. All human motivation arises from a longing for transformation. But there are several different kinds. When you're thirsty and take a drink, you've transformed your condition. If you're poor and hit the lottery, you've transformed your circumstance. But if you're Mr. Scrooge waking up on Christmas morning a totally new man, then you've just experienced a transformation of being.

All three types of transformation are necessary, but when we try to replace one type of transformation with another, we get into trouble. Food, drugs, alcohol, and sex produce transformations of condition, and when used properly, they have their place. It is only when we mistakenly use them as a substitute for a transformation of being that things go terribly awry. The 'rush' of drugs may feel like self-transcendence, but as every addict ultimately finds out, it is merely the gateway to hell... so much of the emptiness that we feel individually and collectively is the result of trying to substitute a transformation of condition and/or circumstance for the transformation of being that we really want."[14]

---

14 *The Business Secrets of The Trappist Monks*, by August Turak

# AUTHENTIC VULNERABILITY

As THE SUMMER moved on, Jason slowly got out of his funk, at least when it came to selling. Seeing a post from Kaiya on Instagram or a Snap story about her going to the movies with Trey still made him angry, but he kept reminding himself what Russ had said: "If Kaiya is who you say she is, she'll recognize what you see in that guy anyway. Good things take time. If you truly care about this girl, you'll hang in there. You'll put in the work doing the little things."

Just like last year, Jason felt things really click into place during the last three weeks of the summer. He'd made a lot of progress as a salesman, though he didn't necessarily know if he had the numbers to back it up. Just like last year, he had made a promise to Russ to 'stop counting' and not look at the scoreboard. He felt like that was a little easier this year than it was last year, which made him happy. Maybe he was learning to focus on the process after all.

But when he finally did look at that scoreboard, he had logged only 90 more sales than last year. Not only did he miss his goal for this year, he barely hit his goal from last year!

He couldn't figure it out. He had put in the work this year; he had pounded the stone day and night. Or so he thought. Sure, there were ups and downs just like last year, but he genuinely thought he had really improved as a salesman. He had even bragged about it on social media, logging a series of posts with the hashtag #hustlelife throughout the summer.

And sure, Jason knew that social media wasn't real life, but it was easy to get caught up in it. He liked flipping back through his posts from the summer and seeing the lineup of shots showing him logging sales and delivering books to smiling clients in his button-down shirt and pants. He liked that version of himself. Looking at the posts, it was easier to believe that version, than it was to face the reality: that despite his progress, he still wasn't where he wanted to be.

So even now, he couldn't resist one last #hustlelife post, grabbing a shot of himself at the bank, holding a big wad of cash. As he was playing with the filters for it before dinner, Russ noticed.

"What have you got there?"

"Just a picture for Instagram." Jason didn't admit he had already spent ten minutes trying to find the perfect filter.

"About how much money you made this summer?"

Jason reddened with embarrassment. "Is there something wrong with that?"

"At the end of the day, I don't care that much about what you post, I care about your heart. What is going on in your heart that you feel you need to post that?"

"What do you mean...?"

"What I mean is that often times when we are feeling inadequate or not good enough, we will try and project an image of success or things 'looking good' in order to try and cover up our true feelings. A king, a queen, or any truly powerful person never needs to tell you they are powerful, they just are. When I was in my 30's I struggled with this a lot. To create that image of success, I wore designer clothes and drove a Ferrari. I had worked very hard to build a significant brand and I wanted other people to know how successful I was. But as I've already told you, inside I was a mess. Every day I desperately tried to cover up my own feelings of worthlessness."

Russ went on, "A picture is just a picture, Jason. It often isn't even reality. But I know I don't have to tell you that. You've experienced it in ways far more painful than words."

Jason nodded, overwhelmed by a sudden wave of sadness. He remembered just last summer, looking through Travis's Instagram and thinking he was living the perfect summer. But he knew now how much of a total lie each picture was, and that the entire time Travis was struggling with never feeling 'enough.'

"Comparison isn't just the thief of your joy, Jason: it can be the thief of your life itself. And what scares me is that you have it much worse than Jan and I did growing up. You all are constantly bombarded by the highlight-reel lives of kids your own age. Some of it is real, but most of it is Photoshopped, filtered, and edited to tell a very specific story. In some cases the cars, cash, and girls are all props that have been rented to make a person look like something they are not.

*The irony is that this 'fake it till you make it' tactic is the exact opposite of how truly successful people live. They live with authentic vulnerability, because they know that the world always connects more with your grit than your shine. They might show up for the shine, but they will stay because of your grit."*

Jason looked a little confused. "What do you mean by grit in this case?"

"I once heard a woman named Sherri Coale talk about how she needed people's grit or else they were too slippery and there was nothing to hold onto. If you look too perfect – which none of us are – then people have a hard time identifying with you. They identify with what's real. To me it's about showing people your scars, your wounds, and being authentically vulnerable about the real journey. Not just showing the highlight reel of your day, summer, or life."

He looked in Jason's eyes, "I'm really proud of you, and I know how hard you've worked and how much you've sacrificed and invested to earn that money. It didn't come easy. But do you really need a picture to prove anything that you haven't already proven to yourself?"

It was a good question. Finally, Jason shook his head, "No, not really."

Russ continued, "We all love being around people who are comfortable in their own skin. People who are so big on the inside that they make everyone else feel big around them. People who are small on the inside try and make other people around them feel small.[15] They almost only want to talk about themselves. They diminish others' accomplishments and inflate their own. They aren't very much fun to be around. And I should know. For the first 45 years of my life, that was me."

"So that's how you learned all of this?"

"Unfortunately, yes. On the outside it looked like I was really big, but that was just to hide how small I felt on the inside. I have spent the last two decades shedding all the layers of junk I put on playing the comparison game and desperately trying to prove that I was good enough, valuable enough, and big enough to deserve love. 'Perfect' is a trap, Jason. And I'm afraid it's one that your friend Travis fell into."

---

15 Came from my notes on a Judah Smith talk.

# CHAPTER 41

# A ROUGH START

JASON'S JUNIOR YEAR didn't exactly start off as well as he had thought it would.

After a summer of pounding the stone every night on the practice court, Jason was excited to get back to a real one. But that excitement vanished as basketball season approached, and an announcement went out that Coach Michael wouldn't be returning for the season. After Travis's death, a follow-up from the school administration revealed that his coaching style may have been a 'contributing factor,' and he quietly stepped down.

Now, the school had hired a new interim coach, Coach Lloyd. He was older than Michael, and rumors were that he only got the job because he was friends with A.D. Miles. And while he had decades of coaching experience, it was in a much smaller school, in a different league.

As much as Jason didn't like Coach Michael, at least he knew him. And at least Michael knew how to use Jason best in the schemes they ran. This new guy was a total question mark. No one knew anything about his coaching style or the kind of program he would run.

"Who knows, maybe he'll be better than Coach Michael." Jason heard that a few times as he and the other guys got ready for warmups and tryouts.

But after tryouts, any thought of enjoying a better season disappeared. It wasn't that Coach Lloyd had a different coaching style than Michael; he just didn't seem to know how to coach at all. He basically just rolled the balls out and let the guys play. He walked the court with a blank look, carrying a clipboard covered in diagrams and notes (though he never communicated what was on it.) He seemed more like a baby-sitter than a coach. Coach Michael might have been a transactional jerk sometimes, but at least he had a high basketball IQ.

Jason introduced himself and did his best to make sure Coach Lloyd knew what kind of player he was, but it didn't seem to matter. In fact, after the first practice, Coach Lloyd began subbing Jason out for someone else for half the practices moving forward. After the first week of practices, Jason felt more confused than ever. How was he going to play for a guy like this?

He knew that his junior season was an incredibly important one for him as a prospect. This was the season he'd planned to make some headlines and get noticed by scouts. But that would be impossible if he was only on the court half the time. And even when he did get playing time, Coach Lloyd had them running such weird systems that Jason felt unused and overlooked.

He felt like he was playing with handcuffs on.

It didn't help that things between him and Kaiya were strange, too. Even after talking to Russ and Jan about it for what seemed like all summer, he still didn't quite know how to deal with her dating Trey. He avoided her for the first few weeks of school, but she must have noticed.

"Jason? Why are you avoiding me?" She found him at his locker between classes. And while Jason thought she looked prettier than ever, he had never wanted to talk to her less. How could he tell her the truth? It hurt so bad.

So instead he just stammered a weak excuse, "I'm not avoiding you. I've just been super busy."

"So busy you can't return a text? So busy you walk around the other side of the building to avoid me during third hour?" Jason tried to argue but she saw through it. "Look, if this is because I have a boyfriend now, you can be an adult about it. Just because I'm dating someone doesn't mean we can't still be friends." Those last words felt like a dagger.

"Yeah," Jason nodded. "I guess so."

"Plus," she added with a smile, "Ryan's been asking to shoot hoops with you again."

That did bring a small smile to Jason's face, but it clouded over. "Why don't you take Trey to shoot hoops with him?"

"Because Ryan didn't ask to hang with Trey. He asked for YOU."

Jason grinned, "Well... maybe you should listen to him about who you date. He's a smart guy."

"Ha ha." Kaiya just rolled her eyes, but as they made plans to hang out with Ryan again, Jason walked away feeling genuinely happy for the first time in a long time.

# PERSPECTIVE

THAT HAPPINESS PASSED quickly, though. The next few weeks were tough.

He felt disengaged from life, with no energy and barely enough will-power to get out of bed each day. It probably didn't help that he'd begun smoking up again every once in a while with Riley and Aaron. Jason wasn't as close to them as he was to his teammates, but he had a complicated relationship with basketball right now.

For the first time in his life, playing ball felt like work to Jason. But not in the way that practice was hard and boring – even then, he knew that what he was doing would pay off on the court in games. This was different. Even playing in games wasn't fun any more. It felt like he was just going through the motions. And for a guy who had only ever loved every second of game time he could grab, that was a very strange feeling.

He wasn't the only one, either. It seemed like the whole team was suffering from that same kind of "loss of heart." Guys were basically sleepwalking through practice, and Coach Lloyd's confusing style wasn't helping. In actual competition, they melted down, losing their first three games. Everyone blamed everyone else for their mistakes, but most of all they blamed Coach Lloyd. It was a poisonous environment for a locker room, one Jason had never really experienced before.

And one night after another big loss, he realized why.

He was the last guy in the locker room, and as he packed up his bag, he looked at the locker across from his. That was Travis's locker. Sadness grabbed his chest. A year ago, he was in this very same spot, laughing and talking to Travis. And that's when it hit Jason just how big a difference one person can make. Travis really had been the heart of the team: he always eased the tension between players, and he always took responsibility if it meant everyone else getting along. He was the glue that kept them all working together without fighting each other. And now that he was gone, the hole he left behind was filled with pain and conflict.

Jason shook his head, wishing his friend was still there. What a difference a year made.

As he left the locker room, he felt like the weight of the world was on him. This was supposed to be his big season, but instead he was playing scrap minutes on a team that was 0-4 and dropping faster than a rock. Worse, he didn't seem to care that much about it. Nothing really seemed to matter anymore. He sighed. The only happy thought in his mind was that at least he got to see Kaiya and Ryan the next day.

Ryan was even happier to see Jason than the first time. He hugged him tightly, then started to race around the court, talking a mile-a-minute about the "new moves" he'd learned. Jason helped him run a "practice" and told him stories about his practices with T.D. over the summer. Ryan's eyes would grow wide and he would just laugh with delight, "SO COOL!"

He stopped halfway through when he remembered that Jason could dunk, and it was a repeat of the last time as Jason put on a dunk show for Ryan. And again, Jason sat to take a breather with Kaiya as they watched Ryan run around with his unlimited energy.

It made Jason happy just to watch Ryan play. And it reminded him of something he hadn't felt all season, and maybe not even since Travis died: that basketball is a <u>game</u>. Ryan had no hope of ever playing for anything other than fun, and yet that seemed to free him up to enjoy it so much more than Jason had all year.

"It's amazing how Ryan's joy and reckless love can help put life into perspective. All the stress I've been going through just melts away when I get to spend time with him. I'm so glad you introduced us, I get now why he is one of your favorite people in the world!"

Kaiya just smiled, "You know, a wise man once said, 'perspective is the only thing that can dramatically change the results without changing any of the facts.'[16] Whenever I'm with Ryan, I get a huge dose of it. Which I need some weeks more than others."

"Yeah, it's got to be a lot of pressure being so cool." Jason shot her a smile, as she laughed.

"You know what I mean. So many things that *feel* like they matter so much in the moment, don't really matter at all. Not in the grand scheme of things, anyway. Once I get perspective, whatever I'm worried about or insecure about right now usually just seems silly."

Jason just nodded, silently thinking about perspective, and feeling incredibly grateful for friends like Kaiya and Ryan who helped provide it for him.

---

16  The wise man is Andy Andrews

# CHAPTER 43

# CONTROL THE CONTROLLABLES

IN SPITE OF his amazing time with Ryan, Jason still had to face the reality of his situation on the team. The hard truth was that he was playing for a coach who didn't know what he was doing.

That became painfully obvious during the sixth game of the season where it seemed like they might actually have a shot at winning. They were only down one, and with only ten seconds left, Jason knew exactly what they needed to do. He had always been a clutch guy in these situations, since he was such a great mid-range threat. All game long, he'd been juking the other team's big man and getting easy layups.

So when they huddled up at the sideline, he smiled excitedly to the shooting guard, "K-Jay, hit me inside. If I get it in the paint, I'll put it away." K-Jay nodded, but then --

"No, no. Hold on." Coach Lloyd shook his head. "Jason, you're out. Eric's going in."

"What?! Are you serious?" Jason couldn't hide his surprise. Eric was a smaller shooting guard, and while he was certainly quick, he wasn't usually the go-to guy in situations like this.

"Yes Jason, I am serious. Who's the coach here?" That was one of Lloyd's favorite sayings, and it had never made Jason angrier than it did right now.

He shook his head, "Fine. You're the coach, but you have to listen to me—"

"See, that's the thing about being coach, Jason: no, I don't."

The whistle blew, and Jason sat down. He watched in blind anger. Just as he'd thought, the play Coach Lloyd had designed didn't work. Eric flubbed a pass, the ball was stolen, and instead of watching his team win, he watched the other team score again to seal their victory.

Jason didn't open his mouth for the rest of the night. He knew that if he did, he was too angry not to say something stupid. He couldn't believe this idiot was his coach.

As he walked out of the locker room, he spotted Russ waiting for him. He nodded to Jason. "Your mom called me, said you needed a ride home."

Jason shrugged, sullen. "Sure."

As Russ drove, he asked a simple question: "Jason, how many of the things you're angry about right now are within your control?"

Jason just sat there frustrated at his situation. Russ went on, "Can you control your coach and his decisions?"

"I wish."

"Can you control whether you win or lose?"

"Yeah, if I was on the court!"

"Wrong. Whether you win or lose is not controllable. You want to believe it is. Everything you've been taught and led to believe tells you that it is.

141

But that's a lie. Jason, our society is obsessed with winning and losing, but you can't control that. Our society is obsessed with natural ability, which people love to call "talent," but you can't control that either, which makes it incredibly overrated. It takes no natural ability to:

> Show up early
> Stay late
> Ask for help
> Give your very best
> Study game film
> Study highlight film
> Dive for loose balls
> Take game shots from game spots at game speed
> Train hard
> Work on mental training
> Treat people really well
> Have powerful body language
> Focus on getting better
> Use beneficial and constructive self-talk
> Keep pounding the stone in the face of adversity
> Be coachable
> Communicate
> Be a great teammate
> Bring great energy
> Always hustle
> Do the little things well
> Be patient
> Persist."

"OK, OK, I got it! You really wanted to make a point, huh?" Jason shook his head at Russ.

"Oh, I can keep going! I know you have a thick skull!" Russ chuckled.

"Nope, I got it. Natural ability is one small piece of the puzzle and you can't change it, so there's no use wasting energy worrying about it. Winning and losing are uncontrollable so it makes no sense to spend time worrying about those things outside of my control, when you just gave me a list of 99 things that are inside of my control that I can focus my energy on."

Russ looked at him with a proud fatherly smile. "So you <u>were</u> listening!"

After finally getting a smile out of Jason, Russ became serious again, "In life you are going to come across challenging situations in the forms of people who are serving as teachers, coaches, bosses, even parents sometimes, but the truth is that you still have a choice to focus on the controllables. You still have a choice to determine the meaning you are going to give that experience. A lot of kids your age quit every time they experience a hard coach, or even a bad coach. But can you see how if you change your perspective and choose to focus on what you can control and lean into it, that it can help you develop the grit and character you are going to need later on in life?"

Jason let out a big sigh as he ran his hand over his face in frustration. "Yes sir, I know you're right. I just wish you weren't. It's annoying."

Russ chuckled. "Oh boy do I know it is. I was your age once too, you know!"

# CHAPTER 44

# NO WAY OUT

JASON TRIED HIS best to take Russ's wisdom to heart, and rededicated himself to pounding the stone and focusing only on the controllables each day. He focused on his heart posture, his work ethic, and his effort when practicing. He tried to take advantage of whatever playing time he could get, and surrender the outcomes that were outside of his control. He even started trying to find and say aloud to himself three beneficial things about Coach Lloyd.

But for someone as competitive as Jason, that was all much easier said than done. No matter how hard he tried, the old habits of ruthless comparison with others wasn't easy to let go of.

It didn't help that their rival team, Hudson, was on fire. Jason couldn't go a day without hearing about it, and he knew that Trey was having an amazing season. He'd already broken Hudson's thirty-year scoring record, and was being scouted by big D1 schools. He even posted an Instagram story about going out to dinner with the head coach from UNC to prove it.

Jason burned seeing it. It was bad enough that Trey was dating the girl he liked, but it was almost worse to see him blow up and have the season Jason dreamed that he would have this year. And just like Jason's dream scenario, Hudson's season included a long playoff run that concluded with a state championship victory. But instead of dinners with D1 scouts and state championships, Jason's season ended 4-19, as Midvale missed the playoffs for the first time in six years.

He tried to shrug it off. He knew by now that Russ was right about focusing on the process, not the outcome. But this time, the outcome just hurt too deeply to not care about it.

After the season ended, Jason was in a serious funk. He couldn't focus on school. His daily workouts were half-hearted at best. He had stopped talking to Kaiya at all. He felt like a dead man walking around.

Which is why, when Riley and Aaron asked him to skip class with them to smoke up and hang out at the mall, he saw no reason not to go along with it. He was bored, and being at school just kept reminding him of how badly he'd failed that year.

After the movie, they were in a shop when Jason saw a lineup of watches on top of a display case. The moment he saw the one in the middle, he wanted it. It was the newest in a line of luxury smartwatches that one of his favorite rappers flashed in his last music video. He saw Trey post on Instagram about getting it as a birthday gift a few months earlier. Jason's 18th birthday came and went a week earlier, and he was really frustrated he didn't have someone to buy him something like that.

He looked around and realized that the salesperson was away, helping another customer. The watches were just lying there. The decision almost seemed to make itself. Jason didn't think twice: one slight move, and the watch was in his pocket. He was almost out the door, when --

"Hey, you! Stop!" Jason turned to see an old security guard walking toward him, an angry look on his face. "I saw you take that watch!"

"What? No way, I didn't take anything. You're crazy."

"We'll check the cameras then. Come here—" He pulled out his radio with one hand, grabbing Jason with the other.

Jason didn't know quite how it happened, but something in him snapped.

As soon as the man touched him, he exploded angrily – shoving the guard hard into a display case. Before he knew it, Jason was standing there blinking, as the man lay on the floor, dazed and bleeding from his forehead. Jason realized that he was in some serious trouble. He turned to run, but he turned right into the arms of two more mall security officers.

There would be no way out of this.

# CHAPTER 45

# IT IS WHAT IT IS

SIX HOURS LATER, Jason sat alone in an empty holding cell at the city jail. He had never felt worse in his entire life. Only eighteen for less than a week and his circumstances were already starting to look a lot like his absentee father's.

He had been arrested for assault and theft, and hauled out of the mall in handcuffs while people filmed it on their phones. But as embarrassing as that was, he felt much more ashamed of what he'd done.

Jason always knew that he faced an expectation about who he was based on how he looked and where he came from. He had always done his best to fight that expectation with everything he had. But after all these years, here he was anyway, *just another statistic*. He was looking at two charges and an arrest record that he would have to live with for the rest of his life.

An officer arrived, unlocking the door. "Let's go, kid." Jason got up reluctantly. He knew what waited for him outside, and he almost would've rather sat in the cell for the rest of the night. But he knew he had to face the music at some point.

An hour later, he was released. The District Attorney was standing with Russ. He stared sternly at Jason, "If I see your name come across my desk in the future, I'll make sure you face the maximum for whatever you have done." Then, motioning to Russ, he added, "Once upon a time this man believed in me, and now he believes in you. Prove him right." He gave Russ a smile and a handshake, then he left.

Jason followed Russ to the Subaru, burning with shame. As they pulled out of the lot, he began his stuttering apology, "I'm really sorry, sir. I... I just didn't want to call my mom."

"I understand."

"Thank you so much... And whatever bail was, I can pay you back. I mean it."

"No, you can't."

"Why not?"

"Because I told the D.A. that you had stayed with me the last two summers, that you made a mistake, and I personally vouched for your transformation over the last two years. So he dropped all the charges."

Tears stung Jason's eyes as he realized the weight of what Russ had just done for him. His voice suddenly got very small. "You... you didn't need to do that... I don't deserve that."

"You know something, Jason? You do. You actually do."

Jason was really crying now. He was stunned. He'd never even heard of anyone doing anything like this for anyone he knew. "I don't... I don't deserve it..."

"What you do with this opportunity, Jason, is up to you. I know you are still struggling with not having a dad in your life, and you are still mad at him. But here is the thing. It is what it is. Your dad isn't coming back, and even if he did, he still can't give you what you already missed out on.

*You have greatness inside of you, but you have to choose between it and excuses. You can't have both. The greatness inside of you is buried underneath all your excuses and rationalizations.* Even though you have legitimate excuses and rationalizations, it doesn't change this truth.

*Everyone comes to a point in their life and they have to decide in that moment who they are going to be. Who they are going to become. You can't allow anyone else to decide that for you.* Would it have been nice to have your father in your life, absolutely, but he made his choice and now you get to make yours. You, not him, get to decide who you are going to be. Do you understand?"

Jason nodded, as they pulled up to his house. Russ turned to look him in the eye. Jason was surprised to see that there wasn't any anger there, either: just empathy and love for him.

"Here." He gave Jason a black box, wrapped in matte-black wrapping paper. "Before you go, there's one more thing I'd like to share with you…"

# CHAPTER 46

# WHOLE ON THE INSIDE

Curious, Jason ripped through the wrapping paper, opening the box. Inside was the very same luxury smartwatch that he had tried to steal.

Jason was stunned. "Thanks... but why did you get me this?"

"Well, I know from personal experience how much a watch can mean. When I was twenty-three years old my father passed away from cancer. He wasn't a great father, but one thing he did do was to always show his love by giving me special gifts on my birthdays.

Ten years after he passed away, I had just launched my first business, and it was really taking off. One day I was playing golf with a friend and he showed up with a brand new presidential Rolex. Something about it made me so angry that it nearly spoiled our time together, but I couldn't put my finger on what it was.

The next day the anger turned to jealousy, and I found myself desperately wanting a Rolex. I went to the jewelry store and I found the one I wanted, and it was just over $10,000. I spent three days obsessing over figuring out any possible way to buy this watch, it was driving me crazy.

Then, Jan had a brilliant insight that unlocked why this meant so much to me. My obsession with that watch wasn't really about the watch at all:

it was about me missing my father. You see, the business I launched was one we had talked about when he was alive, and after just turning 30 having launched that business successfully, I just knew he would've gotten me a Rolex.

Once I realized this, I finally felt free to surrender that watch.

Now Jason, I have never prayed for outcomes in my life. I don't ever want to treat a relationship with God like He is some kind of divine vending machine. But I have a hard time explaining what happened next. I never prayed for the Rolex. In fact, I had been surrendering the stupid thing every morning during my gratefulness prayer and meditation so I could get back to purposeful work.

But the next day, I got a call from my publisher, telling me that a large order was just placed for one of my books, and the check was in the mail. Sure enough, it arrived the next day. I opened it, and couldn't believe my eyes: the check covered the Rolex including taxes and insurance. Never before or after did I have an order for one of my books that was anywhere near that size. It felt as if God was saying in that moment, 'I'm your dad, and you aren't missing out on anything.'"

"Whoa..." Jason's wide eyes landed on the worn Rolex on Russ's wrist. "Is that it?"

"Sure is. I even had it engraved, see?" Russ slipped it off, turning it over to reveal an engraving on the back plate. *'Love, Dad –7/6/85'*. Russ went on, "Now, the point of that story wasn't that getting a watch can fill the hole in your heart. It's actually the opposite. But I understand why you stole the watch, and I'm here to tell you that you aren't missing out on anything either."

Jason looked down at the watch. It seemed foolish now. "Yeah, I know that now. It's just... when I saw Trey get it for his birthday; it made me really sad that I didn't have a father who would get me gifts like that."

"I know you're still trying to fill the hole inside of you that was left by your father's wounds. The truth though, is that no thing, or achievement, or human relationship can fill that hole. Only when you experience, understand, and fully embrace the reckless, unconditional, and scandalous love of your creator will you ever feel whole on the inside.

You don't have to believe me Jason, but you also don't have to look that hard to find a lot of people becoming more and more frustrated and lost by trying to fill that hole we all have with achievements, stuff, and fallible people. A wise man once said, the idea of "*go out and get what you want---and you'll be happy*' is a failed experiment. You can never get enough of what you don't need."[17]

"I've learned that stuff only leaves us with a desire for more. Achievements only give us a temporary high, and then leave us feeling even more empty. People eventually let us down, because they are human just like we are. I got this watch for you so that you will see for yourself how little it will change. It might make you feel good for a week, or maybe a month, but it won't last."

As they got out, Russ gave Jason a crushing hug. "You know that I love you Jason."

Jason nodded, awkwardly. "Yeah."

"Good," Russ nodded. "But you still have to pay off the watch."

---

17 The wise man is Matthew Kelly

"Wait... really?"

"Yes, really."

Jason shifted. "Okay. It might take me a while, though. It's worth a lot of money."

"Oh, I know," Russ grinned. "I guess you might even need a summer job."

Jason sensed what he was getting at, and smiled back. After the season he'd just had, the thought of jumping into a summer playing AAU ball wasn't one that he was genuinely excited about. Plus, he knew his mom needed the money, and he still hadn't beaten his first-year goal of selling 1,200 books. He also knew by now that the process is what mattered, not the outcome; but that's why he didn't just <u>want</u> to do this. He <u>needed</u> to.

He had pounded the stone going door-to-door for the past two summers: he needed to do it again for a third.

# CHAPTER 47

## NO SHORTCUTS

JASON STARTED HIS first day of his third summer selling books with a whole new strategy. Instead of going door to door to individual houses, he planned to only sell to businesses or larger potential buyers like libraries. Why waste time selling one or two or five books at a time, when he could sell one or two or five <u>dozen</u> instead?

Jason mapped out a list of all the biggest potential clients in his territory and started there. And for the first week, it worked. He sold dozens of books each day, logging more orders in his first week than he had in his first month last summer. As much as he heard Russ's voice in his head telling him to "focus on the long game and who you become," Jason couldn't help smiling at the end of each day. It just felt good to be selling this many books!

But then, the numbers began to drop off. It was like everyone had suddenly decided they weren't interested in buying books anymore. Jason knew better than to freak out. He expected bumps in the road. So he adjusted his strategy, and began targeting mid-level businesses and smaller libraries. He re-structured his pitch to be less about the value of a bulk purchase, and more about the value of the books themselves.

Again, this worked for a week or so. And while he wasn't selling as many as a couple weeks before, the numbers were still decent.

Then, again, his sales hit a brick wall. And this time, there was nothing he could do to jumpstart them. After a week and a half of striking out completely, Jason started to worry. He was now five weeks into the summer, and while he wasn't keeping count, he sensed that he was probably already behind his numbers from last year at this point.

Desperate to crack the problem, Jason stayed home from basketball practice one night. He covered the kitchen table with papers, reading through his notes from this summer and the last two. Still, no solution emerged.

"Looks like you could use a hand." Russ looked over his shoulder, studying the papers.

Jason shrugged, "I can't figure it out. I hit a wall."

As he explained the situation to Russ, a smile grew over the older man's face. "Jason, you're falling for the oldest trick in the book."

"What? What do you mean?"

"You know the story of the tortoise and the hare, right?" Jason nodded. "Then you already know the trick. The trick is believing that shortcuts work. That simply by going fast in leaps and bounds, you can get to the finish line first."

Jason shoved the papers away from him in frustration. "But it makes sense! If I sell to bigger buyers, even if I make less sales I'll still sell more books total."

"Are you sure? What do the numbers say?" They did some quick multiplication and division, and Russ showed Jason his projected sell rate for the summer. "Still think it's a good idea?"

As he entered the total, Jason's mouth dropped open. The numbers didn't lie. At his current rate, he was set to sell even <u>less</u> than last summer.

"Most people lose because they are trying to take shortcuts. But there are no shortcuts. Do you know why Michael Phelps is the greatest Olympian of all time? He never took a shortcut. He once went five straight years, 365 days per year, without missing a workout. Can you imagine the willpower, grit, and discipline it took to do that? And it paid off. He won one of his gold medals by less than one hundredth of a second.

I know I've said this to you before, but Jason, talent is so overrated. It's the little things done consistently and remarkably that make the actual difference.

According to data from the National Sales Executive Association,

48% of people in sales never follow up with a prospective client.
25% of people in sales stop after the follow up contact.
12% of people in sales stop after the third contact.
90% of people in sales make no more than 3 contacts.
2% of sales are made on the first contact.
3% of sales are made on the second contact.
5% of sales are made on the third contact.
10% of sales are made on the fourth contact.
Over 75% of sales are made somewhere between the fifth and twelfth contact.

How much talent does it take to follow up with someone over and over again?"

Jason shook his head, "None."

"Exactly. *There are no shortcuts to sustained greatness. It takes what it takes.* If you don't believe me, watch this." Russ opened his iPad and brought up a video on Youtube called, "Speed | A Gary Vaynerchuk Original."[18]

After the video finished, Russ said, "Gary is one of the world's most successful entrepreneurs not because he's faster in his day-to-day execution, even though that's world-class. He is who he is because of his world-class <u>patience</u>. Just like Michael Phelps, he knows that there are no shortcuts. He understands that it takes five, ten, twenty, or thirty years to truly build what he wants. He is completely committed to the process, because he knows that it takes what it takes.

I heard you listening to John Legend the other day. Did you know that it took him twenty years to get a record deal?"

Jason was shocked. "No way!"

Russ continued. "It's true. He started playing the piano at four years old and publicly performing at six. It wasn't until just before his twenty sixth birthday that he got his record deal. Long after he believed he deserved and was good enough! He too talks about the importance of staying true to the process and being persistent."

Jason nodded in stubborn frustration, but he did understand.

"I promise you Jason, *building anything that is sustainably successful, whether it's a great marriage or a career in business or sports, only comes from developing the character to make the patient, long-term choices instead of the short-term ones that are driven by instant gratification.* Most people will take shortcuts instead of doing the work. But the truth is that those shortcuts are really just dead ends or detours. Why?"

"Because," Jason answered with conviction, "There are no shortcuts."

---

18 *Warning: Explicit Language

# CHAPTER 48

# PLAYING PRESENT

At 9 a.m. the next morning, Jason stood in front of his first door of the day refocused and ready to put Russ's wisdom to use.

"*There are no shortcuts...*" he reminded himself. Then, almost like a prayer, he repeated the last line of the Stonecutter's Credo: "*...yet at the hundred and first blow it will split in two and I know that it was not that blow that did it, but all that had gone before. Pound The Stone.*"

With that, he knocked, and the door opened. The call went well; the woman bought three of the books for her kids, and two for herself.

Jason smiled as he walked out; five books wasn't a lot, but it was a start. As the day wore on, he found a rhythm, repeating those words to himself before every sales call. By the time the day ended, he realized he had sold fifty-six books. It was a good start, but he was determined to do better. He wanted to make the most of his time; maybe he could start earlier.

The words echoed again, "*...it was not that blow that did it, but all that had gone before.*"

The more blows to the stone, the faster the stone would crack. As the days passed, that really started to make sense. Learning to focus on excellence in each step of the process no matter the outcome, certainly felt as repetitive and mind-numbing as hitting a rock with a hammer time and time again. But with every sale, he could feel that rock wear down a little bit more.

He just wished it would wear down faster. No matter how often he tried not to think about it, he knew the end-of-summer deadline was coming. That motivated him to sell faster, but it also had a big side effect. It was something Jason didn't even notice until one night at the dinner table.

"Jason? Where are you?" Jan snapped her fingers in front of his face.

Jason blinked, startled. It almost felt like he was waking up from a dream. "Sorry, what? I spaced out there for a minute."

"You did a lot more than that. You've been on autopilot since you got home tonight. You've barely said a word to either of us."

Jason realized that she was right. He apologized, "I've really been working hard. I know how much time I have left this summer, and I just want to make the most of it."

Jan nodded, understanding. "Tell me something, Jason. Where is your mind right now: the past, the present, or the future?"

Jason shrugged. "I don't really know. Probably the future."

"Hmmm" Jan's face crinkled up. "Well, the only place we truly exist and the only thing that is guaranteed is the present moment. What I have found is that if I get caught up in the past or future I actually miss out on the only real thing, which is this moment right now. I think your friend T.D. calls it 'playing present.' I just try and remind myself to be here now, and not let any moments pass me by that I will regret later on. *Regret is poison, so be here now.* The past is gone, and the future is impacted by what you do now."

Jason struggled to grasp it. "So, what can I do to 'be here now'?"

Jan smiled, "I'm glad you asked. Being present is a skill that takes time to develop just like anything else. When you catch yourself not living in the present moment, take three deep breaths, and then feel your feet on the ground. Start to direct your focus inward and feel what your body is feeling. You start with feeling your feet on the ground and listening to your big deep breaths, then you direct your focus outward to the people around you. Really see them. Listen to them. Be there with them."

"Huh. Seems strange, but I'll try it out." Jason replied.

"I hope you do. This is really serious stuff. Everything in our life suffers when we're not playing present. And with technology occupying the place it does, it's harder than ever to be present with those we love. This can lead to isolation, depression, and a whole other list of issues. Maybe that helps explain that while our quality of life in the United States has risen, so have the numbers of people on antidepressants, and the number of suicides, especially among young people. And unfortunately, over 80% of those deaths are young men.[19]"

Jason was stunned. He felt a pang of sadness as he thought of Travis, nodding, "You've got my attention. I'm really going to work on this."

---

19 https://www.cdc.gov/violenceprevention/suicide/youth_suicide.html

# CHAPTER 49

## HUMBLE & HUNGRY

As HE LEARNED to "play present" in his sales, Jason noticed it helped on the basketball court, too.

He had always counted the minutes during practice, as if that would somehow make time go faster. Instead, this always seemed to slow time down, which just made Jason angrier, and it became a loop of frustration where his impatience only made the practice feel longer.

But now that he was learning to live fully in the present and let go of both the past and the future, time seemed to almost disappear. *Once he was fully focused on the moment, and on doing the small unremarkable things with remarkable excellence and consistency, he actually wasn't aware of time much at all.* Whole practices flashed by and before he knew it, he had put in a solid two-hour session. Unintentionally, Jason had created an environment ripe for slipping into what psychologists call a "flow state," and he was experiencing it more and more during training.

All his training was really paying off, too.

The first time Jason really noticed it was after a pickup game in the courts at the park. He had mostly stuck to practicing alone like T.D., but occasionally he would join Smokey and the other guys for a game. If Jason were honest with himself, he still had a chip on his shoulder from that first wipeout game he played against them two summers ago.

Now that he was playing at full strength, it was usually an even match. But this night was different. Jason was playing on a different level, like he had found a gear the other guys didn't even have access to. He drained every shot, breaking ankles all night with dizzying displays of footwork, leaving Smokey cursing as he single-handedly gave his team six wins in a row.

On the last possession of the night, he couldn't resist showing off, unleashing a vicious euro-step and – WHAM!! Throwing down the hardest dunk of the night yet.

Seeing the open-mouthed looks on the guys' faces, Jason got a little cocky. Talking trash and all up in Smokey's face.

He laughed, but realized that everyone else had gone totally silent. Confused, Jason turned around, and froze as he saw – T.D. was standing there, watching. He had seen the whole display.

Jason flushed with embarrassment. Even though he knew he had earned the right to celebrate, something about what he had just done rubbed him the wrong way now that his mentor was here. But T.D. didn't say anything about it. Instead, he just walked up, grabbed the ball, and smiled at the guys. "Y'all need one more?"

Everyone was in awe to be playing ball with this legend, and they quickly chose sides. And as soon as Jason saw T.D. choose to join Smokey's team, he knew exactly what was going to happen next. That didn't make it any easier though.

For the next hour, T.D. took Jason to school. He put a beating on their team that made Jason's own success earlier that night look tame in comparison. Jason realized within one possession that for all of their time practicing, he had never once seen T.D. play like this. The man practiced

162

harder than anyone on the planet, but this was a whole other level. Jason felt like he was playing against Superman.

And by the time he collapsed to the court after the final humiliating basket and scoring zero points, the lesson had sunk in painfully. When the game was over T.D. humbly and politely bumped fists with everyone on the court, and instead of gloating in his own success, he thanked them for playing.

Afterward, he and Jason walked back toward the house in silence. Finally, Jason worked up the courage to speak, "Thanks for that. I get it now."

Slowly, T.D. smiled. "I hope so. You know Jason, the byproduct of great-ness isn't ego: it's humility. The best in the world always have a healthy, humble respect for the game and their opponent. *You want to always stay humble and hungry. There is always more to learn and always room to grow. Mastery isn't a destination, it is a continual process and never ending journey.*"

# CHAPTER 50

# 10,000 DOORS

As JASON ENTERED the final month of the summer, he began a practice of doing early-morning conditioning before work. The endless sets of sprints reminded him of those 5 a.m. practices he put in sophomore year to make the team. Except that this time, while he still didn't exactly love conditioning, he was doing it for no other reason than now knowing that the pain of discipline was much better than the pain of regret. Every time he found himself on his hands and knees gasping for breath, he reminded himself of that principle.

He found that starting each day with a hard workout gave him an edge in sales, too. He was sharper, more focused, and in a better mood to start the day, which helped kick things off. He sensed that it was getting easier to focus on doing the little things, though it was difficult to tell.

His days going door-to-door began to blur past, blending together with the nights he spent on the court. The feeling of flow got stronger and stronger. After two years of training, doing T.D.'s fundamentals routine, it had been seared into his memory. It had become instinctive, a part of himself, as natural as breathing.

This familiarity with the whole routine allowed him to "zoom in" and focus on perfecting even the smallest motions of each drill. He felt this pay off in his footwork most of all, as his natural agility and rhythm became supercharged by the relentless hours of deliberate training he had put in.

He felt like he had unlocked a new power-up in a video game. Movements that had felt awkward and foreign to him at first were becoming second nature. Of course, some days were tougher than others, but Jason really thought he was starting to see some progress from all of his work.

"Sounds like you found the sweet spot," Russ smiled as Jason finished up his dinner one night. He had been talking nonstop about how much fun he had had that day between selling books and putting in a hard workout.

"Yes, sir, I guess so. The weird thing is," Jason continued, "I realized this morning that I haven't 'checked the scoreboard' all summer. I honestly have no idea how many books I've sold."

Russ exchanged glances with Jan. "It's funny you should mention that."

Jan smiled, "Because we got a call from your program director today, with some exciting news."

"What is it?" Jason was curious.

Russ paused, and then, he spoke very straightforwardly: "Well, for the first time, you might actually want to check that scoreboard, son."

Jason couldn't get another word out of Russ, so he fired up his laptop and checked his sales figures on the company website. When he saw the number, he thought it was a mistake. He blinked and looked at it again. It couldn't be right. But there it was: 2,592.

Jason couldn't believe it. That was more than double both his past summer's numbers. He shook his head, blown away. Russ shook his hand, man to man. "Congratulations, Jason. You've come a long way."

Jan wrapped him in a warm hug. "We're so proud of you, Jason."

Jason swallowed a lump in his throat, and just said, "Thanks." Then he grinned to Russ, "Looks like I won't have a problem paying off that watch after all."

"I never doubted that you would. Not for a single minute."

It was a nice way to end Jason's final year of selling books. And while he was tired to the bone from the work he had put in, he knew that he would actually miss the job itself. He had grown to truly love the process of going door to door. He had grown to love that it wasn't easy, that success wasn't guaranteed, and that every single door was a totally different opportunity to develop more character and grit. He had probably knocked on 10,000 doors over the past three summers, and that unrelenting process had sharpened his natural abilities into something much more focused and professional.

By the time he knocked on his last door, he did it knowing that no matter what the future brought, he had 10,000 doors-worth of experience behind him now, and he was that much better equipped to face anything the future held.

# CHAPTER 51

## "BE A MAN."

On Jason's last day at Russ and Jan's, Russ told Jason that he had a surprise for him. They got into the Subaru, and drove into the city, where they pulled up to what looked like an old-school barbershop. The sign over the door said, "Atelier di Gianluca."

As they walked in, Jason quickly realized it was a tailor's shop. There were a few racks of incredibly-cut suits, as well as several in-progress suits on mannequins.

"Russell!" An old Italian gentleman bounced toward them, greeting Russ like an old friend.

Russ introduced him as Gianluca, his tailor. "He's been dressing me for thirty years. And now, he's going to dress you. He'll be making a custom suit for you."

Jason looked at him in surprise, "Whoa, Russ. I... I don't know if I can afford that—"

"Don't worry, Jason. This is my gift to you, no strings attached. Call it a graduation present."

Jason thanked him, mind blown, as Gianluca bobbed around him, tape measure already out, talking excitedly. They picked out a fabric, and after taking Jason's measurements, he told him the suit would be finished in a few weeks.

As they got home, Jason couldn't believe how generous of a gift this was. He only had one suit, and it fit about as well as a garbage bag. The suits at Gianluca's were the opposite, each one crafted with mastery, excellence and classic Italian flair.

He couldn't stop thanking Russ, "Thank you so, so much!"

Russ just smiled at him, "You're very welcome, Jason. You've become a man now, and every man needs at least one great suit."

Something about those words hit Jason in the heart, and he blinked back a flood of emotion. Russ noticed his reaction, concerned, "What's the matter? Is something wrong?"

"No, sir. It's just..." Jason took a deep breath. "The only two times I've seen my dad, the thing I remember him saying to me wasn't 'I love you' or 'good job.' It was 'be a man.' And I don't know why, but... if I'm being really honest, I just never truly felt like a man. Until you said it now."

"I'm so, so sorry to hear that, Jason," Russ replied, a look of deep concern on his face. "'*Be a man*' are three of the most damaging words a boy can hear growing up."

"Why?"

As they sat at the kitchen table, Russ grabbed a pencil and paper. He drew a box on the paper, and labeled it "Be A Man."[20] He then asked Jason to name some of the words that define what it means to be a man in our culture. Jason started to list them as Russ wrote them down.

---

20 Exercise from Joe Ehrman's book, *Inside Out Coaching*

*Tough*
*Strong*
*Stoic*
*Pimp*
*Ladies man*
*Athletic*
*Muscles*
*Domination*
*Power*
*Money*

As he finished, he asked Jason, "So. What are some of the rites of passage boys engage in to prove their masculinity and their right to be in the man box?"

Jason didn't have to think long about that one. "Out-drinking other guys, or partying harder than anyone else. Having sex with a lot of hot girls, having a lot of girls into you at once. Doing drugs, maybe even selling them. Dominating athletically and in sports. Getting in fights."

Russ nodded. "And if you don't fit in the 'Be a Man' box, what do you get called?"

Jason took a deep breath, "A lot of bad words. Weak-ass, pussy, bitch, gay, homo..."

"And if you ever found yourself outside the box, getting called those names, what would you do to get back in?"

Jason shuddered, "Anything. Absolutely anything. It is too painful to be out of the box."

Russ looked at Jason with deep empathy. "I know what you mean. I was in high school once as well. We have created this false narrative around hyper-masculinity and told young boys that is what it means to be a man. Be tough. Never cry. Never need anyone, for anything. Never show emotion other than anger and power. Solve your problems with your fists. Treat women and less powerful boys poorly and make them fear you. I've seen and experienced it all. I bought into the 'be a man' lie for a long time, just like it sounds like your dad did. How did it work out for him?"

Jason nodded. "Not well. He's still in prison."

> Russ shook his head. "It is so sad to me that we've established a culture of masculinity built on shame and turning boys into monsters not men. Real men have courage, especially to take a stand for those who are weak and vulnerable. Real men use their strength in service of others.
>
> Real men are willing to be vulnerable and show emotions. Real men are willing to cry. Real men know that they can't just 'go it alone.' Real men are great friends. Real men develop empathy for others. Real men respect all people."[21]

"Like you do. I've seen you do all of that." As Jason thought back over his friendship with Russ, his thankfulness grew. "Thank you so much for showing me what a real man is."

Russ shrugged, "I've had a long journey to arrive at a healthy understanding of masculinity, what it truly means, and how best to cultivate it in my life. But I'm still learning. You know it was Fredrick Douglas who said, *it's easier to build strong children than to repair broken men.* I have seen this too many times in my life, and I'm grateful I had patience and wise mentors who helped repair me. Not everyone gets that."

---

21 Watch the documentary, *The Mask You Live In*, on Netflix

"Well, you've certainly taught me a lot. I'm so grateful I knocked on your door three years ago!"

"So am I, Jason. You've come a long way." Russ gave him a proud squeeze on the shoulder. "But I will warn you, that to whom much has been given, much will be required. As a senior, you're going to be looked up to this year. You will need to step forward as a leader. You may not be aware of it right now, but your actions have echoes in the halls of your school. What you do matters immensely.

I'm not sure what exactly it's like there, but if your school is anything like mine was, the 'be a man' culture of masculinity is probably pretty firmly in place. But you have the power and opportunity to change that. A lot of people look up to you because of your size and athleticism, and follow your actions and attitudes whether you realize it or not. If you have the courage to live out what it actually means to be a man, people will follow. How cool would it be if you created a culture and left a legacy that changed what it meant to be a man in your school?"

Jason realized how powerful that really would be. "It would be pretty amazing."

"The opportunity is there, Jason. I trust you'll take advantage of it."

# CAPTAIN

WHEN HE FINALLY made it home, Jason slept for almost two days straight. He had never been more exhausted in his life. But he had also never been prouder or more focused. He knew this was a big year, and he wasn't going to let it get away from him.

As he was out buying a new pair of jeans the day before school, Jason realized something really surprising. He had been focused so intensely on work and practice that he had barely even thought about Kaiya all summer. It really surprised him. He had spent so much of the past two years thinking about her, that to know he hadn't done it in a long time was kind of shocking. He thought about texting her, but didn't. He was certain their paths would cross at school again soon enough anyway.

And he was right. The next day, there she was in his Government class. He was worried it might be awkward, but she gave him that beautiful smile. "Saving me a seat, stranger?"

After class they caught up, and Jason quickly noticed that she seemed really happy and more like herself. She had spent the summer working as an intern at SpaceX in California, and she had loved every minute of it. She rattled on and on, and by the time they'd reached Jason's next class, she stopped herself, "I'm sorry! I didn't even ask how your summer was. Want to grab some coffee or something soon? I was rude, so I'm buying."

"Sure," Jason nodded. "Long as it's cool with Trey."

Kaiya shook her head. "Don't worry about that. We're not together any more."

"Really?" Jason tried not to sound too excited. "That's, ah... that's too bad."

"No, it's not. And you know it." She smiled and her eyes twinkled a little at him. "See you tomorrow."

Jason couldn't stop smiling the rest of the day. For once, it looked like there might be a chance with Kaiya.

Jason knew from experience that the *Slight Edge* principle of building habits was a double-edged sword. The path to mastery meant doing things that were easy to do, but also easier <u>not</u> to do.

He didn't want to waste the process he'd gotten used to over the summer, and so starting the first week of school, he kept it going. He showed up at 6 a.m. to the gym, and got his conditioning in before the day began. The same focus and edge he felt in kick-starting the day like that was the same for school, too. At least, it helped him pay more attention in class for the first half of the day, which had always been a problem.

Jason knew that his training had been slowly paying off over the summer, but it didn't quite hit him until he played his first scrimmage against his own teammates. These were guys he had played with for years, and while he was more athletically gifted than many of them, his lack of technical ability and refusal to practice had always evened it out a lot.

But that had changed.

Jason seemed to have leapfrogged everyone in a single summer. He was faster, his shooting more accurate, and his footwork was more effective.

"Man! Who'd you ball with all summer, Lebron?" Mike was their best player at guard, and he couldn't stop whooping after Jason used a move that he had developed all summer to split the defenders, loft in an easy layup, and jog halfway down the court by the time they knew what had happened. He used it a half-dozen times before they caught on, and even then all he had to do was switch hands to have them swinging at air all over again.

When everyone asked him what had changed, he just shrugged it off, "Just a lot of pounding the stone." Any time he was tempted to brag or get cocky, he remembered T.D.'s harsh lesson about staying humble and hungry. They were still a long way from the season, anyway. He still had plenty more work to put in.

But he wouldn't be doing it alone. The second week of school, Jason showed up for his usual 6 a.m. conditioning and saw that Ray, their center, was already there waiting. Ray gave him a sleepy nod, "Yo Jase. Wanna show me what you do? I want to start putting in that extra work..."

Jason showed him the simple workout he had learned from T.D. As he expected, Ray was surprised. "Really? That's it?" But after Jason reassured him that this was really the workout he had been doing for the last three summers, he just nodded and went along with it.

Two days later, they were joined by K-Jay, one of the other guards. He, too, wanted to see what Jason had been doing that led to his edge on the court. Just like Ray, he was surprised at the simplicity of the workout, but he didn't complain or walk away – instead, he just joined in.

He wasn't the last one, either. Before tryouts had begun, the core group of seniors were putting in an extra hour and a half of work before school started, pounding the stone along with Jason.

This was such a massive change in the team dynamic that the day tryouts started, Jason was called into the coach's office.

There he learned two things: one, that Coach Lloyd had been let go, thankfully. And two, that he really liked his new coach, Coach Brant. This guy was calm, cool, and collected, and Jason could tell immediately that he cared just as much, if not more, about the guys on his team than he did about winning. It was clear from moment one that they would get along.

Brant told him that he couldn't believe what he'd been seeing out on the court. "Is this the same team I've read about? I was under the impression that things weren't going so well last season."

"They weren't," Jason admitted. "But things are different now. Just watch."

As tryouts progressed, his words proved true. It was obvious to all of them that this wasn't going to be just any season. Something had clicked into place. Many of the seniors had been playing together for almost a decade now, and after the confusion and disappointment of last season with a bad coach, there was a maturity there that was missing before. That core group of the team had been through fire together with losing Travis, and Jason's transformation truly inspired many of them. They were focused and dedicated in a way not many teams their age were, and it showed.

Before the season began, it was no surprise to anyone that Jason was unanimously chosen as captain for the squad that year. Jason was honored, but he knew that a title wouldn't change anything. Above all, he and the team needed to focus on one thing only this year, and that was pounding the stone.

# CHAPTER 53

## FINALLY

As EXCITED AS he was about basketball, Jason was even more excited about Kaiya.

Their 'quick catch-up' over coffee had turned into four hours together of laughter and joy, as Jason told her all about the summer, with all of its victories, defeats, and lessons. There was a point in the conversation where he noticed something strange. She was looking at him in a way that she never had before.

Kaiya noticed him staring. "What's the matter?"

"Nothing, you're just looking at me different now."

"Well, maybe because you <u>are</u> different. And don't worry, that's a good thing."

"Why? How am I 'different'?"

Kaiya scrunched her face up, like she was admitting something. "I don't know, you're just not the same guy you have been. There's no more chip on your shoulder. It's like you grew up. Your arrogance has turned into something more like real confidence. It's very attractive."

"Over the summer?"

"I know, it sounds weird. But I think it's true." Kaiya smiled.

Jason dropped his head. "Well, there's a reason for that, and it's not pretty. I actually got arrested for shoplifting and assault. Russ bailed me out, and told the D.A. I would be living and working all summer with him, so they dropped the charges. But it really shook me. My whole life all I wanted was to be different from my dad, but I ended up behind bars, just like him."

Kaiya nodded, overcome. "See, that's what I mean. The cocky kid I met a few years ago never would've had the courage to share that." She reached over, and she gave Jason a big hug.

Later that night after they'd said goodbye, Jason walked home thinking about it. It certainly felt true. He did feel like he was finally more comfortable not just with who he was, but with what he had learned, what he had been through, and where he was going. It wasn't anything like the cocky feeling he had always tried to put off, but something much deeper and heavier. It was real, genuine confidence, and he knew the reason it was there: he had pounded the stone for the past few years. That process built more than just skill at selling or playing basketball: it built courage, authentic vulnerability, a growth mindset, self-awareness, patience, a heart posture shift, and real grit. For the first time in his life, Jason could finally trust the man in the mirror.

And that confidence told him it was time to finally put it on the line. He knew that what he had with Kaiya was special. It wasn't like anything he'd ever felt for a girl before, and he wanted to make it real. He just didn't quite know how.

He'd never had a problem getting girls to go out with him; that just always seemed to happen easily. All he had to do was text something like 'yo, you want to hang out?' and things would go from there. But he knew Kaiya, and he knew she deserved better than that.

"What you're talking about is being direct, Jason. Being honest and direct about how you feel is a huge part of being a man," Russ told him. "A man doesn't half-step around what he feels and wants. If you'd like to ask this young lady on a date, do it. There's nothing magical or fancy about it. Tell her how you feel, and ask."

Jason knew Russ was right, but that was so much easier said than done. He had to do Jan's "being present" exercise of three deep breaths and feeling his feet on the ground about four times before he was calm enough to ask Kaiya. When he finally did though, the smile on her face had never been brighter.

"Yes, I'd love to!" She replied.

Their date was amazing, and as Jason walked her to her door that night, he still couldn't stop smiling. He couldn't believe he was dating a girl like this. Because to him, he knew that there simply *was* no other girl 'like this.' Kaiya was her own woman, with more ambition and bigger dreams than anyone Jason had ever met. It was clear that just as it had for him, the past summer had really made a difference for her.

He didn't know what their future held, but he couldn't be more excited about it.

# CHAPTER 54

# GOING FIRST

As BASKETBALL SEASON approached, Jason was adjusting to his new role as captain on the team.

There had always been someone else up the ladder above him, and after a lifetime of that, he wasn't used to being looked up to. It added another dimension to everything he did and said. People modeled their own actions after his, and that was kind of scary.

But there were exceptions; not everyone looked up to him. In particular, Anthony, one of their talented sophomores, simply didn't listen to Jason. He didn't show up to their early conditioning sessions, and he was always the last one to follow any directive coming from Jason.

It was really beginning to slow down the team's effectiveness, too. Jason got sick and tired of Anthony messing things up that would be easily fixed if he would listen to Jason or respect his role as captain. He was an immensely gifted athlete, but his 'go my own way' attitude was hurting the team and even worse, it was spreading. A few of the underclassmen thought it was funny, and began to side with Anthony on things.

Jason tried talking to him one-on-one and on the court, but nothing seemed to get to him. He just laughed or shrugged it off, clearly too cool to care.

Jason's frustration boiled over one practice, and he caught himself screaming at Anthony, using language that could have come right from

Coach Michael – lots of shame-based name-calling. He apologized to the team afterward, but it really rattled him. That wasn't the way to lead, and he knew it. But he didn't know what to do. So of course, he called Russ.

"So, being team captain isn't all it's cracked up to be?" Russ smiled at him across their usual booth at the local diner.

"No way!" Jason shook his head. "At least, not when you've got a guy like Anthony on your team. I mean, I'm trying everything I know to get this guy to fall in line, but nothing's working. And I know it's not my fault or anything, but it still bothers me—"

"Are you sure about that?"

"What?"

"You're the team captain. Are you sure it's not your responsibility?" Jason didn't answer, confused. "There's something I think you should watch. Here."

Russ brought up a video on his phone, and handed it to Jason. It was a TED talk by one of the most intense men he'd ever seen, a former Navy SEAL Commander named Jocko. He shared a devastating story from the Battle of Ramadi in Iraq, where the men in his command were engaged in a friendly-fire incident that killed and injured their own soldiers and allies. Jocko's boss arrived the next day, and asked him in front of his whole company, 'Whose fault was this?' One after another, his own men took ownership for the various things that had gone wrong, but every time, Jocko told them it wasn't their fault. Finally, he looked at his commander and said, 'It's my fault. I am the commander, and I am responsible for everything that happens on the battlefield. <u>Everything</u>.[22]'"

---

22 Extreme Ownership, by Jocko Willink, TEDx University of Nevada, available on YouTube

Jason blinked, realizing that he was both intimidated and inspired. "Whoa."

Russ nodded, "If you expect people to follow you as a leader, you have to take extreme ownership of everything in your world. That means having to ask yourself the question, 'What if Anthony's attitude is my responsibility? What if it's a result of something I'm doing or not doing?'"

"Yeah, I think I get it. But even if I find out what that thing is, how does it help make him fall in line? He acts like he's not accountable to anyone but himself!"

"He's not."

"What do you mean? Are you saying I shouldn't hold the guys on my team accountable?"

"Yes, that's exactly what I'm saying. You must climb the mountain yourself, then call them up to the level you're living at. Lots of leaders like to call people *out*, hypocritically I might add, but very few are willing to go first and then call people *up*…. step by step by step.

If you want to lead well, you have to go first, and you have to call people up."

"Hmm," Jason thought about it. "What exactly does that mean? I'm always the first in the gym and the last to leave, and I always try to help guys that need it during practice."

"Well, that's a great start! But, how authentically vulnerable are you being with them?"

"What do you mean?"

"Jason, that mask we talked about living behind as a man is much easier to wear if you're a leader. We're conditioned to believe that a leader should be strong, stoic, and certain of everything. If vulnerability is seen as weakness, then a leader must by definition be the most invulnerable person in the room. How many leaders have you known like that?"

Jason flashed back to the coaches and teachers he'd had, realizing, "A lot!"

"The irony is that human beings know that vulnerability requires deep amounts of courage, because being vulnerable requires opening yourself up to the fear of rejection and shame that you have to face by allowing yourself to be seen and known. Real strength isn't being invulnerable. It's being strong enough to overcome the fear of vulnerability."

"If I remember correctly, you and Anthony have a lot in common from your first couple of years. Maybe you need to share some of your journey with him, and admit a lot of the things you were struggling with as a freshmen and sophomore."

Jason's face scrunched up. He sighed deeply, "I hate admitting it, but we do have a lot in common."

Russ smiled. "It's amazing to me how far you have come that you can own that. That in and of itself is huge progress for you. Now you just need to focus on being authentically vulnerable with the guys you lead while simultaneously going first and calling people up!"

Jason gave Russ a big hug, "Sometimes it sucks talking to you, but I know it's good for me. Thank you for caring enough to tell me the truth with empathy."

# COURAGE IS CONTAGIOUS

THE NEXT WEEK, Jason called a 'mandatory captain's meeting' for the team.

"Look, I want to talk about something that has affected all of us: losing Travis. I know it's been over a year since it happened, but not a day goes by where I don't think about him. And I know that a big reason last season didn't go as well as it could, is that we never really talked about it. And since… well, since we're the guys who knew him best in a lot of ways, I think it might be valuable for us and honoring to him, to talk this stuff out."

He saw the whole group of guys get tense. He knew this would happen. His heart pounded, and for a second he thought about bailing on the whole thing. But Russ's words rang in his ear, 'you have to go first.' So he swallowed his fear and kept going.

"I don't know about you guys, but losing him really messed me up. Like, bad."

He paused, the words catching in his throat. He suddenly noticed that everyone's eyes were on him. A few of the guys were even nodding. Even Anthony was silent, like he was waiting to see what Jason was going to do next.

What he did, was share. Honestly. Openly. It was the first time he felt like he had actually been truly emotionally honest with someone his own age about what had happened, and it felt really good. It was weird at first, and hard, but as he kept talking, it got easier, and things he had never told anyone before, or even realized himself, came out. It was the first time Jason had ever cried in front of his peers.

Before he could even finish speaking, Mike raised his hand. Jason nodded to him, and the big guy cleared his throat. "Is it ok if I go next?"

One by one, each of the guys shared from the heart about Travis and how losing him affected them. Some stopped there, others used it as a jumping off point to share other things on their minds and hearts. Jason was amazed, and felt a thrill of real friendship with his teammates. There was something great about doing this together – no coaches, no teachers, just them. He now knew why Russ had advised him to do this with his team members only. There was a freedom to share with each other that just seemed easier.

As they shared, Jason felt something incredible happen: it was like a weight was lifted off the entire team. Like the elephant in the room that hadn't been talked about for over a year was now out in the open. It felt so good.

Finally, only one guy remained: Anthony, who had kept a stiff upper lip the whole time. While Jason interpreted this as his usual 'strong, silent' act, once Anthony spoke, it was clear that Jason had really misread him. There was no trace of ego now. This was genuine, from the heart.

"Travis came to my house one night, a week before he died. And I know we all looked at his life and thought it seemed perfect... well, there was a reason for that. He said all his parents cared about was that everyone saw how 'perfect' they were. The house, cars, clothes, vacations, 'loving relationships,' and best of all, him. The perfect son. He said he felt like a schizophrenic sometimes, like he was living two totally different lives: his real life, and the life he showed the world. He said that life felt like a mask, like 'happy' was just a word in a dictionary, not something that was possible in his life any more."

Anthony cleared his throat, his words thick with emotion. "He said it was getting harder and harder to keep wearing that mask each day. His mom had bulimia and OCD, and his dad had an affair last year that almost destroyed the family. But they never told anyone, because then some- one would know that they're not perfect. He said that's why he tried so hard at everything he did. Every good grade he got, his achievements in sports, getting into a good college... he thought if he performed well enough, he could hold it all together.

But he was worried it wasn't enough. He didn't get into the schools he wanted, and he knew they were bitterly disappointed by that. He said they just told him, 'What will we tell our friends?' and then they started talking about how their friends had kids who got into this college or got this scholarship. They made him feel completely worthless.

They expected perfection from him, but he was giving it everything he had, and he just didn't have anything else to give. He was never good enough, and he felt like he was just letting them down by being there. But he had no way out. He didn't have a voice, he didn't have a self other than that mask he had to wear. Then, he said... 'I know one way to take it off for good, but I don't want to do it.' I asked him what he meant by that. But he just said, 'Nothing. I'm just venting, you know?' Then he made me swear not to tell anyone. He tried to play it off, like he was just really stressed about school."

A sob tore through Anthony's voice, "I should have known. But when he said that, I believed him. He was just always such a happy guy. But the day he jumped, I was there, in the crowd, and I overheard his dad on the phone in this really low voice. He wasn't crying or anything, he was just saying, 'What's everyone going to say? What will they think about us as parents? This will be in all the papers...' And I knew then that Travis was telling the truth." Anthony shook his head in grief. "If you ask me, the guy didn't just jump. 'Perfect' pushed him."

Around the room, heads nodded. Jason was blown away at the depth of feeling and insight displayed by Anthony.

He looked him in the eyes, man to man. "Thank you, Anthony. That was powerful, man. I didn't know you went through that, and I'm so sorry you felt like you couldn't bring it up. I'm sorry for any of my attitudes as a captain that might have added to that. But I want you to know that I care about you. <u>We</u> all care about you. You don't have to carry stuff like that alone. We're all in this together."

Anthony just nodded, silent again, but it seemed like he accepted it. Jason stepped across the circle and gave him a strong hug, thanking him again for sharing what he did.

The rest of the meeting passed without Anthony saying much else, and Jason wondered if this moment of vulnerability was a one-time thing. But at the next practice, he could tell something had changed for good. The chip was off Anthony's shoulder, and he seemed lighter somehow. Without any prompting, he was really digging in and running every drill with the same focus and intensity as the other guys.

Leaving practice, Jason couldn't stop smiling. Russ really was right: courage is contagious.

# CHAPTER 56

# CHANGING THE ECHOES

JASON WAS LOVING everything about his senior year so far. But it wasn't long before Russ's words that "to whom much has been given, much will be required" were proven very true.

One day, Kaiya was late to their meetup at her locker. Jason could tell immediately that something was wrong. Her eyes were flashing with anger, as she told him how she'd spent her last tutoring session of the day with Steven, a really bright freshman, one of her favorite tutees.

"I could barely get him to talk about it, but it sounds like he's getting bullied pretty badly. He had to leave his last school because of a similar situation, and he's had a hard time making friends here. Jason, I'm really worried about him. I could tell he was in a pretty dark place today. I asked if he wanted to go to the counselor, but he just said he's 'fine.' No offense," she told him, "but sometimes I really hate the way guys behave."

"Yeah, so do I. They're pretty stupid sometimes."

"Real men don't need to make others feel small in order to make themselves look big. It just makes me so angry that a couple of guys think they can do that just because they wear letterman jackets. They walk around like that somehow entitles them to be jerks."

"Wait a minute. Letterman jackets?" Kaiya nodded, as Jason's anger grew. "Are they basketball guys? Guys from *my* team?"

"He wouldn't say. I think he's worried that if he says anything, it'll just get worse."

Jason nodded, but he felt an alarm going off deep in his spirit. He remembered Russ's words, *"your actions have echoes,"* and the lesson of taking extreme ownership as a leader played back in his mind. He knew something had to be done. Kaiya must have noticed.

"Jason? What's going on? You look like you want to punch something."

"I do. But I know that wouldn't do any good. Solving problems with your fists just feeds that same 'be a man' lie that created this situation in the first place. Still..." he trailed off, his mind speeding, "Something has to change. Do you know which lunch period he has?"

She told him, then asked, "What are you going to do?"

Jason paused, thinking. Then, "I'm going to go change the echoes."

The next day, Jason entered the crowded cafeteria and scanned it looking for Steven. He noticed how divided everything was, the distinct order of social status plotted out by table. He waved to a couple of his friends, who motioned for him to come over and sit with them. But instead, he wove through the tables to the opposite side of the cafeteria, where Steven sat eating alone.

"Hi Steven, is it okay if I eat with you?" The younger boy looked a little unsure, but he shrugged. Jason sat next to him, and started eating and talking to him. He never mentioned the bullying, but just got to know Steven as well as he could, treating him as he would treat any of his friends.

He felt the eyes of the whole cafeteria on him, and after a while a few of his friends actually came over and joined them. He introduced them to Steven, and they all carried on the conversation. Steven didn't say much, but by the end of lunch, he smiled at Jason and said a quiet "Thanks" before walking off.

But that wasn't the end of it. Jason was intentional to include Steven in his conversations or to say hi to him in the halls, and he ate at Steven's table each day. It seemed like he was slowly opening up to Jason, getting a little more comfortable each day.

And it helped that, true to Russ's words, Jason's actions and example really did 'echo.' He never explained anything to any of his teammates, or called a big meeting to talk down at them about bullying – instead, his actions did the talking. Jason started looking for people who looked lonely all over the school and would ask them their name and find out what they were interested in.

Any time one of the guys asked him why he went out of his way to include Steven or some other random person, he just explained the 'be a man' lie, and said that he was doing his part to reverse that culture at their school. They always walked away with funny looks on their faces, but he noticed Mike and K-Jay begin following his example and reaching out to or including a few other kids who normally went unnoticed or were usually picked on.

A few weeks later, Kaiya walked up to Jason, glowing. "I know what you did for Steven. He hasn't mentioned anything about bullying in the past few weeks, and today, he told me about how he's so grateful for his 'friends at lunch.'" She wrapped her arms around Jason, kissing him fiercely. "Thank you, for being a friend when he needed one. Thank you for being a real man."

190

Jason just smiled. "Don't thank me, thank Russ. I know I have a long way to go, but he's taught me a lot about what it means to be a real man."

# CHAPTER 57

# RESISTANCE

JASON'S SHIFT TOWARD authentic vulnerability and a more authentic life in general meant a big difference in his words and actions, and he noticed that he had begun to live life with a lot more clarity and power. While some people in his life were incredibly supportive of these changes, there were many who weren't; specifically, Riley and Aaron, the guys who'd been with him on his fateful trip to the mall that ended in an arrest.

Any time they saw each other in the halls or in class, Jason couldn't help but feel like something had changed. They were colder to him, and one day they even made fun of him for choosing to practice on a Friday night instead of go to a huge party with them.

"What's the matter, Captain? Can't take a night off? What'd you do with Fun Jason, huh? We liked that guy..."

When Jason told them he couldn't, they got even worse. "Whatever, man. You're too good for us, that's fine."

Jason was surprised. They treated him like he'd betrayed them. But just last week he had texted both of them to hang out. No answer. He suspected that since it didn't involve alcohol or drugs, they ignored it.

When he told Kaiya about it, she just nodded, "Yeah, get used to it. Have you ever heard of the 'crab mentality'?" Jason shook his head, he hadn't.

"If you put one crab in a bucket, it will crawl out. If you put multiple crabs in a bucket, they will pull each other down every time one starts to crawl out. If a crab continues to try and crawl out of the bucket the other crabs will break its leg."

"Whoa. That doesn't make any sense at all!" Jason responded.

"Just like it doesn't make any sense for Riley and Aaron to make fun of you right when you're really taking some amazing steps of transformation. Even though the man you're becoming is a much stronger, more capable, more empathetic person, they'll fight that transformation every step of the way. Because every step is like a mirror for their own insecurities and shortcomings. You guys grew up on the same block. And if you can change, it means that they can too, if they only had the courage and discipline to consistently choose to do so. But they would rather believe that they're the victims of their circumstances, and that change is impossible, because that means they can go on living how they have been and not think about it. Change is scary, and you shouldn't be surprised when some people in your life resist it, instead of celebrate it."

"Wow," Jason shook his head. "I guess I never thought of that, but it makes a lot of sense. You talk like you've been through that yourself?"

"Well, you have some idea now that you're going through the same thing. But girls can be a lot worse than guys. They make everything a lot more personal. When I started my tutoring business I experienced social shame like you wouldn't believe. At first, when I started taking responsibility for my life, instead of worrying about my hair, nails, and boys, most of my 'friends' completely abandoned me. Then they started shaming me and ostracizing me at every opportunity."

Jason looked shocked. "I'm really sorry to hear that. That's awful."

Kaiya just smiled. "That's why I read a lot, and the more stories I read of people who have done the things I want to do, I realized most of them experienced way more shame and persecution. They even burned Joan of Arc alive. So, I learned that *there are no extraordinary people, just ordinary people willing to experience shame, persecution, and even death to pursue what sets their soul on fire.*"

Jason was amazed at Kaiya, and was so grateful he had put in the work to develop the character and become the type of man she would want to spend her time with.

# CHAPTER 58

## SWEEP THE SHEDS

BY THE TIME basketball season began, Jason was in the best shape of his life. Months of pounding the stone, both alone over the summer, and together with his team once school started, had paid off. He had come a long way from the guy who hated practice just a few years before.

After his 'take off the mask' meeting with the other seniors, the team was even more in sync than ever. Everyone showed up each morning at 6 a.m. to put in their hour and a half of conditioning and training, and each night after practice, Jason stayed late to keep shooting. And even though he still didn't love them, each day he ran through T.D.'s footwork and fundamental drills, pushing himself harder and harder each day.

The season had an uninspiring start, going 2-3 in their first few games. Jason had to admit he was disappointed, but he didn't let it show. Instead, he kept repeating – both to himself, and to his guys in the locker room, "Relax, and trust the process. Focus on what we can control, the meaning we give the experience and what we do after it. We just have to keep pounding the stone."

His words calmed everyone down, and proved to be prophetic.

The next game was a breakout game for Jason. He was unstoppable, going 12 for 14 from inside the paint and draining a pair of threes on top of that. He was perfect from the free throw line, finishing with 38 points on top of ten assists and thirteen boards. A triple double, the holy grail in basketball. On the last play of the game, he even unleashed his now-signature ankle-breaking split-the-D-to-dunk move, sending the crowd to their feet in wild applause. Jason had never been more excited after a game. After the past few years of pounding the stone in the dark, he was finally feeling like all his sacrifice and persistence were paying off on the court.

Afterward, he encouraged the other guys: "This is only the beginning. Trust me."

Again, those words became true as the team went on a blazing hot run of 12 more wins. Every time it seemed like they couldn't score any more, they would break that record the next game. Jason led the team in scoring and assists, and he couldn't deny that it felt great to be recognized for it, too. Out of anyone on the team, he had put in the most time pounding the stone, and it made sense that he would be that much further ahead of everyone else.

Success is a double edged sword though. For the first time in a long time, as the excitement surrounding the season grew and there were more demands on Jason's time, he began to practice less. Some of the best schools in the country had started calling and texting him every day, and more people were asking for his time. It started with a half-hour of extra sleep here and there, as Jason showed up later and later for their morning practices. He knew he was letting things slip, but he knew it wouldn't matter. The Raiders were unstoppable. HE was unstoppable.

But not for long.

Eventually, they lost a game. Then one more. Finally, in the most confusing night of his entire history on the court, they tanked what should have been the easiest win of their season, dropping a huge 43-77 L to last-place Ellsworth, one of the few teams they had beat last year.

Jason was stunned. That night, it was like playing on a completely different team. Their timing was off, everyone was blaming each other, and Jason personally felt like his mind was disconnected from his body. He was completely in his head the whole game, overthinking everything. It was the wrong type of out of body experience. He couldn't hit any of the shots he usually did, and felt like he had two left feet for most of the game. He didn't know what exactly, but something was very wrong.

He stayed in the locker room until well after everyone else had gone home. If he were honest, he simply didn't want to take ownership of his own shortcomings, and face the embarrassment of speaking with the reporters who he had been bragging to for almost two months now.

Jason heard the door to the locker room open, and was surprised to see Russ walk in. The older man simply nodded his greeting and sat down next to Jason. "You know, you've got a very concerned girlfriend outside asking about you. Thought you might have fallen in the toilet and drowned." Russ smiled.

Jason shook his head, "Feels like I did."

"What happened out there tonight?"

Jason hesitated. He knew exactly what had happened. "It wasn't tonight, actually. It's something that's happened over the past few weeks."

"Which is what?"

"I stopped putting in the work that got us here, and the team followed suit."

"Why?"

"We got used to winning. It didn't feel like we needed to."

Russ grinned, "Well, you know how I feel about living by principles instead of feelings. Now you know why."

Jason nodded, taking that in. Suddenly Russ shifted, his eyes lighting up. "Jason, can you name the sports franchise with the highest winning percentage in human history?"

Jason puzzled, "Um... the Yankees?"

"No. In fact, it's not an American team."

"Ah... huh. Maybe the Brazilian national soccer team?"

"They're very dominant, but that's not the answer." Russ shook his head, "The answer is the *All Blacks*, New Zealand's national rugby team. Over the course of recorded competition, they have won 83% of their games."

Jason's mouth dropped open, "Shut up... that's insane."

"Yes, it's definitely pretty astonishing. But what's more astonishing is the fact that despite this, they have a legendary reputation for being by far the most genuinely humble team in sports.

The craziest thing is that after any match, even a World Cup final, you will find the best players sweeping the locker room and cleaning up after everyone. They have a radically different philosophy than many of our western teams, and it doesn't just show up with clean locker rooms. Their heart posture ends up showing itself on the scoreboard as well. When you ask them why they have been so successful, one of the first things they will point to is their culture of 'Sweep The Sheds'."[23]

---

23 *Legacy: What the All Blacks can teach us about the business of life*, by James Kerr

Russ looked around the locker room, "so what do you say we stop sulking, and start cleaning this place up?"

# CHAPTER 5 9

# WHO DO YOU WANT TO BE?

JASON TOOK THOSE words to heart, and threw himself back into practicing harder than ever. He was determined to embody the heart posture of 'sweep the sheds' as well as possible, and to never let winning derail him from pounding the stone ever again. That determination paid off, as he and the team got back into their groove again, and began to find their rhythm once more.

They squeezed out a win, then another. Things began to feel more normal, as they kept winning.

But while the practice was paying off on the court, it affected other parts of Jason's life in ways that weren't as positive. He was constantly tired, and he found it difficult to focus in class sometimes. He found it more and more difficult to 'play present' off the court, and even spaced out while he was with Kaiya, which hadn't ever happened before. It didn't help that he had to start thinking seriously about his after high school plans. Jason felt the pressure to make the right decision.

One night as he was hanging with Kaiya, it hit a breaking point.

"Jason?! Are you even listening to me?"

Jason snapped out of his thoughts, realizing that Kaiya had stopped speaking about 20 seconds ago. "Yeah, sorry, I'm just really stressed. Got a lot on my mind. You were talking about something at your work?"

"Yes, I had a breakthrough with Carissa, the girl with dyslexia I've been working with."

"Oh, that's good, right?"

"Yes, Jason. That's good." Kaiya's eyes flashed, "So. What's on your mind that's so much more important?"

Jason knew she was under a lot of pressure as well, but he couldn't help firing back, "Well, we have the year's biggest stretch of games coming up and there are rumors that even a few NBA scouts will be there. So yeah, it's a lot to think about. But sure, let's talk about tutoring instead."

"Excuse me?!"

"I'm just saying. It's not like that's going to pay off the way basketball will."

Jason regretted it the moment it came out of his mouth. But there was no taking it back. Instead, he had to just watch it land on Kaiya's beautiful face, as the words pierced her heart like an arrow. Her face crinkled in pain, as emotion rose in her eyes.

"Wow," was all she could say. Jason started to stammer out an apology, but she cut him off. "No, you've said exactly what you mean. I'm glad I know what your priorities are now."

She gathered her things and walked out, leaving Jason stunned and silent. He thought about chasing after her, but he shrugged it off. He was angry at her response, though he couldn't say why. "She'll cool off..." he thought.

But the next week proved him wrong. Kaiya didn't respond to any of his texts or DM's on social media. He and the team won their next game, but not by much. Jason knew why, too: his head was messed up. He felt terrible about what he'd said to Kaiya, but even his apologies were getting nowhere.

Finally, he didn't know where else to turn so he called Russ.

As they sat at their usual booth at the diner, Russ listened silently, allowing Jason to vent. "--I told her I was sorry too, like a million times! I just wish she got it."

"Got what?"

"The pressure I'm under! I feel like I've been carrying the team on my back the whole season. I've got coaches calling and texting me all day, and we are entering the hardest part of the season!"

Russ paused. "Jason, do you still think this is just about basketball?"

Jason paused, confused, as Russ went on, "Face the facts, son. You've deeply hurt someone you truly care about, all because you're still focused on what? Basketball, a scholarship, pro ball? That's the outcome talking, not the process. You still think that by winning a championship, or making it to the NBA, you're going to be worth more as a person. That's just not true.

It's not about the game, Jason. It's never just about the game. It's about the person you become through it. That is why the process matters, so much more than the outcome.

I once had one of the most respected people in coaching tell me that he wants to see a kid play poorly when he is watching. You know why? Because seeing how he handles adversity will tell him a lot more about how that kid will handle the next level more than anything else.

It's easy to give your best, treat people well, have unconditional gratitude, and have a great attitude when everything is going the way you want. But how will you respond when everything hits the fan? In sports, business, and life it is a guarantee you are going to hit a lot of adversity: that's why it's not about the game. The game is just another place to experience adversity and refine your character. Your character is all that matters. If you miss that, you miss everything.

I knew a guy in high school named Brandon. Brandon was a star athlete, maybe even better even than you. His size and talent were really something special. He was one of those guys who only came along once in a generation. He was being scouted by the NBA as a sophomore. Everyone knew that this guy had an incredible future ahead of him in sports.

But unfortunately, Brandon's character didn't match his abilities. To put it plainly, he was a completely selfish person, all ego and no character. He thought it was funny to make fun of special needs students as he passed by them in the hallways, mocking them and their teachers -- even though many of them were fans of his. People knew this about him, but they let it slide because of his athletic talent.

However, the summer before his senior year, Brandon passed out at the wheel while driving home from a movie after drinking and smoking some weed. His car went off the road and flipped eight times. He barely survived, but would live forever as a quadriplegic who could never move anything but his eyes or mouth again. He could not eat, bathe, or use the restroom without the help of another person.

And so he spent his senior year, the same year that everyone expected him to be fielding offers from various NBA teams, in a wheelchair instead of in the spotlight. And instead of being surrounded by his teammates and beautiful girls, he spent that year in the special needs room, surrounded by all of the kids, who, just a few months before, he loved to make fun of."

Jason was stunned. Russ looked at him with deep empathy and compassion, "Jason, this is why the process matters so much more than any outcome. All the championships in the world are worthless if you can't love people and live with ownership, authentic vulnerability, and integrity. One of my favorite quotes in the world is, 'what shall it profit a man if he gains the whole world, but loses his soul?' So the next time you find yourself caring more about the world than your soul, think about Brandon, and remember the true value of character."

# CHAPTER 60

# THE FUTURE

AFTER SPENDING ALL night tossing and turning as he thought about what Russ said, Jason knew what he had to do. No more texts, no more DM's. This had to happen face to face.

The next morning, Jason drove to Kaiya's house at 5:30am. He brought her favorite drink from Starbucks, and the world's biggest apology. When she answered the door, she was confused, but she accepted the coffee and listened as Jason poured his heart out on the doorstep. He apologized for letting the circumstances get to his head and affect their relationship.

"Because I know I'm not perfect, I can't promise that it won't happen again at some point, but I can promise you that as long as I'm with you, I will never take you for granted like that again. You're the best thing that's ever happened to me, and I know how lucky I am to be with you..."

"Did you know that 'Kaiya' wasn't supposed to be my name?" Kaiya interrupted. Jason shook his head, confused. "My dad is Japanese and my mother is Jamaican, and in her family a daughter was always named for her mother's mother. But when they saw me for the first time, I guess they decided I had to be named after my father's mother instead, Kaiya. Do you know what my name means?" Jason shook his head. "In Japanese, 'Kaiya' means 'forgiveness.'"

Jason felt emotion rise in his chest as she looked into his eyes and smiled. "So, you forgive me?"

She answered him with a long kiss, "Of course I do. I'm sorry I haven't been answering my phone or anything. It was a really tough weekend."

Jason noticed the dark circles under her eyes and realized that he'd been so focused on his apology that he hadn't noticed she wasn't just tired from waking up early: she was tired because she had never gone to sleep. "What's going on?"

Kaiya rubbed her eyes, clearly exhausted. She handed him her phone. "Look at this."

The email was from someone at SpaceX. Jason read it quickly, "...*would be so excited to have you join us again, and are prepared to offer you the same package we do for all of our incoming program members...*" His eyes started skipping over words – "*housing package includes rent at an apartment of your choosing near our facility...*" "*...moving package includes airfare for you and a family member...*" "*...we eagerly await your response...*"

As it clicked, Jason met her eyes, understanding setting in. "You've been thinking about this all weekend."

She nodded, "I'm sorry I didn't reply to you, I know I should have, but I don't know what to think... and I was really trying to process this fully before talking to you."

Jason re-read the email, realizing, "Wait, so this would mean that you're moving to California once school is over?"

"Yes, if I take it. But I'm not sure that working there is what I want right now."

"Why not? I thought you loved that place! And I know how tough of a program it is to get into..."

"I know, but it would mean leaving my tutoring business, just when it's really beginning to grow. I've added five more clients just this year..." She trailed off, her eyes meeting his. "And then there's us. If I'm in California..."

She didn't finish the sentence, but Jason knew what she meant. If she was in California, they might not be together. He cleared his throat, "Look, maybe if I can play ball at UCLA or Cal."

She nodded, but it seemed like her mind was a million miles away. Jason hugged her, "Look, we can talk about this later, okay? I think you need some sleep."

Kaiya nodded, kissing him goodbye. And while Jason was rock-solid in his feelings for her, he was now more unsure of the future than ever.

# CHAPTER 61

# GOING TO THE 'SHIP

EVEN THOUGH THE future with Kaiya was very up in the air, Jason felt so much better now that he had made things right with her.

On the court, all his work pounding the stone was paying off. His fitness was unbelievable. For the next four games, he and the Raiders gritted out win after win, going into double overtime two games in a row to take the division. Jason got stronger in overtime when everyone else's legs looked like they were moving through water. The semis brought even tougher competition, but with Jason leading them, the team was ready for it. The regional final was a blowout, Jason and the Raiders were heading to State.

Before their first game at State, Jason got a handwritten note in his locker from T.D.

*"Keep pounding. I'm proud of the man you are becoming."*

Inspired, Jason shared it with his teammates, and they rolled over their first two opponents. The third game was much tougher, a shootout that they barely put away in the final few minutes. As the buzzer sounded and the Raider fans rushed the floor, Jason realized what this meant: they were going to the Finals... where they found out they would face their old rivals, Hudson.

Jason knew that this would be his biggest challenge yet. He would be playing his nemesis, on the biggest stage and under the brightest lights of his career. College coaches from UNC, UCLA, Texas, and Kentucky would all be at the game. This was the exact scenario he had faced three years ago as a hotheaded freshman, which landed him in Coach Michael's office. Had he grown enough to overcome it?

Before the game, Coach Brant shared how proud of them he was and the men they were becoming. He then wrote on the board:

Focus → On playing for your teammates rather than your shots, feelings, or pain
Fight → For all the little inches
Finish → Empty

"If you do these three things, you will be able to play with freedom and have a lot of fun! Let's go!" Everyone jumped up out of their seats and put their hands in the middle.

Coach looked everyone in the eyes. "You guys have been pounding the stone all season, now let's go out there and finish empty. Finish empty on three!!"

The game started out exactly as expected: evenly matched. Both teams were playing their best ball, and it was quickly obvious that there would be no easy winner here. This was going to be a knock-down, drag-out title fight. The kind you only made it through on grit and sweat equity.

In the fourth quarter, the whistle shrilled for a timeout. As the team gathered at the bench, everyone started talking over each other. But Jason quieted the whole team, holding up a hand. He said simply, "Hey, look: we're down ten points. So what? I don't care if we're down twenty. What do we do, no matter if we're down twenty or up twenty?"

The answer came instantly, from memory, "Pound the stone!"

Jason shot them a smile, his confidence was contagious. "Exactly. Just like we have been all season. I don't know what the final outcome of this game will be tonight, but I do know I am going to pound the stone until the final buzzer sounds. Who's with me?"

The guys shouted their response, energized, and focused by his words.

As the whistle blew and the action got underway again, that's exactly what the Raiders did. Pass by pass, shot by shot, they surged along, unleashing a series of quick scores that brought them within a single point. They were experiencing what the Navy SEALs call merging, where they were no longer operating as five individuals on the floor, but rather as one seamless unit.

But as the clock dipped to two minutes, that's when it happened.

The Hudson guard bricked a shot from the line, and Jason flew in for the board. He ripped the ball from the air, but as he came down, the guy beneath him rotated, tilting Jason, and – POP!! Jason felt his ankle roll like rubber beneath him, overextending as he crashed to the ground.

Jason bit back a scream, knowing immediately that his ankle was badly sprained if not broken.

Complete silence fell as everyone froze. The refs and athletic trainers rushed out, and Jason slowly got to his feet and hobbled to the side-lines. Even the smallest pressure on his foot was followed by searing pain. Behind the bench the athletic trainer did a range of motion test, and then looked to Coach, shaking his head. "This is sprained, or worse. He may have torn a ligament."

Jason saw the realization hit Coach Brant; his star player wouldn't be coming back. He looked Jason in the eyes and shook his head, eyes filled with emotion. "I'm so, so sorry, Jason."

And with that, he called time out to talk with the team as Jason went back to the athletic training room with the athletic trainers.

# CHAPTER 62

# THE STONE SPLITS

As the athletic trainers talked between themselves, the door slid shut.

Jason heard the crowd outside, and he silently wondered how this could happen in the biggest moment of his career. He heard the hushed voices of the athletic trainers. He even heard the rhythm of the cheerleaders trying to jumpstart the crowd in chants as the game got going again. It all felt far away, like he was underwater.

He felt the fiery pain in his ankle, and he pushed away the temptation to start blaming this situation on anyone or on himself. The injury was an accident, nothing more or less. It had happened, and there was nothing he could really do about it now.

As he sat there on the table, Jason flashed back to what Russ had told him so many times: "You're going to go through storms in life, Jason. Do your job so well that you can sleep through them. Can you sleep through the storms, Jason?"

The question echoed in his mind. He had certainly put in his time pounding the stone, but this was no ordinary 'storm.' A torn ligament in your ankle isn't exactly something you can train for, he thought. It's not like you can play basketball on one leg, right?

Suddenly Jason jolted up straight on the table like he had been shocked by a cattle prod.

He couldn't believe he hadn't thought of it before. He got the athletic trainers' attention as he hopped up onto his good leg, a look of pure determination on his face. "Can you tape me up?"

They exchanged confused looks, "You mean like... to go back in and play? Sure, but you're not—"

"Can I hurt it any worse?" He asked with a look of steely resolve.

"No, but—"

"Tape it up now, please. I'm finishing this game." The look in his eyes told them that Jason was dead serious. Convinced, they complied, wrapping the ankle as well as they could. He thanked them both and hobbled back down the tunnel, out to the court.

A glance at the scoreboard told him everything. The Raiders were still down one, with fifteen seconds to go. He made his way to the bench, and a hush fell as people saw him hobbling out. The players all slapped him on the back as he approached Coach.

"Jason?! What are you doing?" Coach Brant looked concerned.

"Put me back in. We can do this."

"Are you serious? You're injured, Jason, I can't—"

"Get me the ball, and I can do what it takes, I promise you."

"How? You only have one good leg..."

Jason replied with iron conviction. "Trust me. I've trained for this."

Coach couldn't believe he was doing this, but he nodded. Something in him believed Jason. He had watched Jason put in countless hours beating on his craft, and that consistency had given Coach Brant a deep level of trust in him. He waved out Jason's replacement, and Jason jogged back out onto the court. He did his best to keep off the injured ankle, but even the few moments of pressure on it were blasts of mind-numbing pain. The crowd rose to their feet and started clapping with a growing roar, the energy going through the roof, like this was the NBA Finals.

Jason nodded to his teammates, who couldn't believe what they were seeing. "Jason, what are you doing, bro?"

He replied simply. "What do we do when we're up ten or down ten?"

The answer came like clockwork: "**We pound the stone**."

"And what do you do when you only have one good ankle and ten seconds left?"

This time they all smiled as they replied, as one, "You pound the stone."

"Exactly. <u>That's</u> what I'm doing," Jason nodded. He looked over to K-Jay, who would be inbounding the ball. "K, just get me the ball, alright?"

K-Jay nodded, smiling. They all knew how insane it sounded to do this, but they trusted Jason.

They took their places, and Jason faltered a bit. The whistle screamed, and everyone exploded into motion. Jason whirled around the pick set by Mike, hopped forward and caught the incoming pass from K-Jay.

At this point, muscle memory took over, and Jason knew that it was his only hope of pulling this off. If he didn't, they would lose this game.

As he caught the ball, Jason faked left – tapping his injured foot to the court – then, pivoting hard, he threw down all his weight on his good leg, as – whoosh! the defender bit on the move, flying past him – leaving him with a totally clear shot.

What happened next might have looked impossible to anyone who didn't know that Jason had spent the last three summers on his footwork. Even then, it was nearly unbelievable. Without even planting his injured foot or shifting his weight, Jason used the momentum of his move to carry him forward and shoot at the same time – it looked like a completely off-balance shot.

As he floated back to the ground, time seemed to expand, and Jason could see the details around him unfolding in slow motion: the tumbling form of the defender who was just now realizing his mistake – the moving figures of his teammates…

*Jason, do you still think this is just about basketball?*

Like it was happening far away, Jason heard the buzzer sound, and he knew that this was it: there would be no second chances. Everything rode on this.

*It's not the outcome that matters. It's who you become in the process…*

A camera flashed somewhere, and in the strobe light he could see the wide-eyed faces of the crowd, every single pair of eyes locked on the ball as it sailed toward the rim – all except for one.

From her seat just above the bench, Kaiya wasn't looking at the ball. She was looking at Jason.

*Surrender the outcome, Jason...*

Behind him, the ball dropped closer toward the basket.

*Trust the process.*

As Jason landed, rather than watching the result of his shot, he locked eyes with Kaiya... and smiled.

# CHAPTER 63

# YOU AREN'T ENTITLED TO YOUR DREAMS

"That was some game," said Russ. It was the next day, and he and Jason sat across from each other in their usual booth at the diner.

Jason smiled, "I'm just grateful you and Jan were able to be there. It was tough, but I drew a lot of strength from having you guys there."

"Have you decided what you're going to do yet?" Russ asked and Jason shook his head no. "Well, either way I'm so proud of the man you have become and will continue to become on your journey! Jan and I have worked hard to try and help you to develop grit on the path to mastery over the last few years, and during this next phase there are a few things to remember.

First, lots of people are going to try and talk you out of things that look impossible. At many phases in your life people will tell you to give up on your dreams, grow up, and get a 'safe' job, even though those don't exist anymore. And if you are just throwing pennies into wishing wells, then you do need to grow up. But if you are earnestly and faithfully beating on your craft and developing the grit needed to live those dreams, then ignore the doubters.

I've found a lot of people who quit on their dreams have a lot to say about those chasing theirs, because they have a vested interest in it really being impossible or only for the talented few. You know by now that this isn't true.

Finally, always remember that mastery is a never ending process, not some destination. The true greats are on a perpetual journey of constant and never-ending improvement. John Wooden was still taking notes and sitting on the front row well into his nineties!

You learned to ride a bike through failure and persistence. Over and over again. The same way you learned to walk and then run as a child. The wisdom I have shared with you over the past three years is no different: you must continue to take what you have learned and act upon the wisdom. You must experiment and fail over and over again as you put the wisdom into practice in your life. It's not good enough to just hear wisdom, or read it, you must perpetually go and learn how it works in the real world by attempting to use it over and over again.

People like Martin Luther King Jr, Mother Theresa, Nelson Mandela, and others like them were not extraordinary people, they were ordinary people who were willing to die for extraordinary principles. They were ordinary people who continued to pound the stone for decades without seeing the stone split. Nevertheless, they persisted.

You have that same power inside of you. You are so much more powerful than you realize.

*Don't ever settle for average.*

*Don't ever settle for easy.*

*Don't ever forget that you only get one life.*

*You aren't entitled to your dreams.*

We need you to pound the stone and develop the grit necessary to push our world forward, more now than ever. Just remember that with every blow from that hammer and every choice you make, you are building your house.

*Build wisely.*

The world is counting on you."

**The End**.

# Thank YOU for reading!

You might have noticed there were more than 7 lessons in this book. Probably more like 70 times 7! The important thing to me is that you pull out the 7 most important lessons for you in your unique journey, and then start applying them to your life. I would love to hear your top 7 ☺

You can also download the Pound The Stone motivational mixtape at t2bc.com

Love,

Joshua Michael Medcalf

Twitter: @joshuamedcalf

Instagram: @realjoshuamedcalf

Email: Joshua@traintobeclutch.com

Cell: 918-361-8611

# Bring the *Pound the Stone* message to your organization

*Keynote*
*Discussion Guide*

*Video Program*
*Offsite Workshop*

Visit www.poundthestone.com for more information.

If you are interested in implementing the Pound The Stone philosophy, lessons, and discussion guide with high school or middle school teams or groups, please contact lucas@traintobeclutch.com He is our resident ninja with implementing the t2bc curriculum with young kids.

*I get asked a lot about the stories and characters in my books and whether they are true stories. Most of the characters and stories are based off of stories and people from my life or other people I have had the privilege of working with. For example, this is the real life Ryan, who I became friends with last year, and I immediately knew I wanted him to be a character in one of my books.*

# More Books by Joshua Medcalf

*Chop Wood Carry Water,* is the story of a young boy named John, who embarks upon a ten-year journey to live his dream of becoming a samurai warrior. Lessons on mental training, leadership, and life-skills are woven into the storyline as John progresses through his journey to fulfill his dream. This story will captivate your attention and help you understand the importance of, and how to, fall in love with the process of becoming great. A quick read at only 120 pages, its simple story with deep themes engage kids and adults alike. When people ask where to start with mental training, we encourage them to start with *Chop Wood Carry Water,* as it will lay the foundation in a super practical way. It is the book I would have given anything to have had growing up.

*Chop Wood Carry Water* is a viral sensation and we are confident that you too will fall in love with the process of becoming great as you go on a journey with John.

We are living through one of the greatest shifts and redistribution of power our country has ever seen. Many people have failed to see that beneath their political frustrations the shifts really have to do with the disruption caused by technology. Casey Neistat has turned down multiple offers from companies like HBO and SHOWTIME, because he generates more views on YouTube than they typically get for their shows. Last year, I turned down a six figure publishing deal, because my book Chop Wood Carry Water was a viral sensation that didn't need a traditional publisher to make a big splash in the marketplace. The tribe I had built on social media gave me the leverage and confidence to be able to say "no thank you." Every day jobs that used to be safe are becoming harder to find or disappearing all together. Then finally, when ESPN announced it was making massive layoffs and it became clear that my kids might grow up without it, I realized just how fast this shift was happening. Much like the guy with Aspergers in The Big Short, I have been seeing how many areas of our economy: education, advertising, media, and entertainment, just to name a few, are being propped up artificially and are a house of cards ready to collapse.

In November of 2016 I gave a keynote presentation at an event in Australia called, *Money In Sport*. I had landed in Sydney, Australia to find out Donald Trump was the next president of the United States. Four days later, I spoke about how the thing I learned from the election was that traditional media's influence is a dinosaur unaware that it is about to become extinct.

I wrote the book, *Hustle*, as my entrepreneurial memoir with all the lessons and failures I learned along the way. In order to thrive, and possibly even survive this new world we are living in, you must learn to think and act like an entrepreneur. In this book, I teach you how.

Many people who have read all of our books believe that, *Transformational Leadership*, is our secret gem. Originally it was released with a different title and for whatever reason it did not sell that many copies. We didn't think too much about it, and just moved on writing new books. But then like a cult classic that flops at the box office, people who were reading it came back to us blown away at what was happening in their life after reading it.

In this book we really try and help people move from transactional leadership to transformational leadership. In the insta-everything world we live in today, it is easy to lose focus on your mission and start treating people like production units instead of treating them like people.

However, this actually undercuts your results, because no one likes to work for, play for, or be around people that don't treat them like people.

In our experience working with founders of billion dollar companies, professional sports teams, division one coaches, and everyone in between, there is a lot of talk about transformational leadership, but not very many people who are living it. Transformational leadership isn't sexy, soft, or easy.

*Burn Your Goals* is the first book we wrote that put T2BC on the map. It is a highly countercultural book that helps people understand the importance of shifting from living a goal driven, achievement driven, life, to living a mission driven life. This book is a tome, but only the first 50 pages focuses on the concept of Burn Your Goals. I get really frustrated at books that should have only been 50-75 pages, but because the publisher requires it, the book continues for another 200 pages. This book is not like that. It combines many other stories and ideas that delve into leadership, life-skills, and mental training.

*"On a quit night in the C-Suite of Axis Medical Group, Brian Kelly holds a ten-pound sledgehammer, standing in front of a massive corner office. Staring back at him is his own name, etched across the door in polished block letters. He worked for twenty-five years to get it there, but tonight that has to change. And so, with every ounce of his strength... Brian starts to swing."*

We're entering an era that will become to be known as the age of the network, a world of hyper-connectivity and constant flux, where disruption is the norm and autonomy, empowerment, and meaning are basic expectations of the new workforce. The challenge leaders face today is the fact that we live in a half-changed world, where everything from communication and etiquette, policies and procedures, where and when work happens, and "paying your dues" are still influenced by a long list of unwritten rules established by the world that preceded the Network: the Hierarchy. Successfully navigating the challenge of thriving in two very different worlds is the mandate of the modern day leader. This book will show you how.

Drawing on their years guiding everyone from Fortune 500 executives to major-league coaches through the new world of work, Seth Mattison and Joshua Medcalf combine timeless wisdom with timely strategy in, *The War At Work*, a fable grounded in two leaders' introspective journey from the top down world of the hierarchy to the hyper connected world of the Network.

If you are like me, when you have a question, you want an answer. When you are unsure of what direction to go, you want someone to lay out the perfect path for you. We spend massive amounts of time in books, articles, videos, courses, and education seeking these answers. No doubt, you hope to find some here. But here's the reality: No book has THE answers.

The answer you need, and will find, is not what you seek. Because it's in our search for answers that we develop the characteristic of accruing wisdom. In becoming someone who passionately accrues wisdom, we must apply wisdom. For, in the application of wisdom, we are transformed. And it's this transformation we undergo in our journey that is truly the answer.

It's not the answer we were looking for, but it's the answer that allows us to be effective in the world and transformational to and for those around us. When you read this book, you will not underline the answers. You will find wisdom and principles to be applied. Apply the wisdom, and become the answer.

# Want to go deeper?

**Mentorship Program**- Our mentorship program isn't a good fit for everyone, but we are always willing to see if it is a good fit for you. It is a serious investment of time and resources. Email Joshua@traintobeclutch.com for more information.

**T2BC Reading Challenge**- People are consistently telling us how going through our reading challenge has radically improved their business, family, and personal life. It is available to download under the *free stuff* tab at t2bc.com

**The Experience**- *Transformational Leadership Retreats.* We bring together people from all over the country to engage in a day of interactive learning. We also create space for fun activities like golf, surfing, or snowboarding with the t2bc team.

**The Clutch Lab**- Our T2BC podcast takes a deeper dive into leadership, life-skills, and mental training.

**T2BC 101 Online Video Course**- With over 20 short video sessions, you can use this course individually or to teach your team the T2BC curriculum. It is a great next step tool. Available at **t2bc.com/training**

**Join the T2BC community**- This is the best way for us to provide consistent value to your life and for us to develop a long term relationship. You will get articles, mp3's, videos, and other tools as they come out. It's also free. Join at t2bc.com

**Books**- If you are interested in bulk order pricing. Please email info@traintobeclutch.com for a custom quote.

**YouTube**- Our channel is *train2bclutch*

# Thank You's

I'm incredibly grateful to my mother, who has supported me and been one of my best friends my whole life. Thank you for never giving up on me when no one would have blamed you if you had.

Thank you to my father, who did the best he could with what he had.

Thank you Judah Smith for being the most amazing pastor a person could ask for. You have taught me so much about Jesus, and how He really feels about me. I don't think anyone has ever had such a profound impact on my life in such a short period of time as you have.

I'm so grateful to Jamie and Amy, you both have been such an amazing support system in my life, and I'm so grateful I get to spend so much time with you. Thank you for creating a safe space for me to be me devoid of judgment.

Thank you Lisa for always being there to hear my articles, or just to listen to another one of my crazy stories, and for being an incredible best friend! Your kindness and empathy are something I hope to one day be able to embody.

Thank you Steph for another brilliantly designed cover, and all you do to make everything we create look way better. We wouldn't be close to where we are today without all your dedication and love you have poured into our brand and all of us.

Thank you Lucas and Katie for making our brand better and helping turn our content into curriculum that impacts young lives at such a deep level. You truly inspire me!

Thank you Seth for being an incredible friend, mentor, and allowing me to be myself and loving me regardless. Your friendship has meant the world to me.

Thank you Russ and Skip for all the mentorship over the years. Thank you Skip for being one of the first people outside of my family to financially invest in me and my dreams.

Thank you Andy and Terry for teaching me so much as a teenager. I wouldn't be here today without your love and wisdom.

Thank you Jacob Roman for helping take my crazy ideas and narrow them down into something people actually want to read. You are the first person who showed me 7 years ago what it means to pound the stone. Thank you for your dedication to your craft. You are a true craftsman!

Thank you Sydney for your love and support and giving me opportunities to grow in ways I didn't think I was capable of. I am proud of the journey you have been willing to embark upon.

Thank you Jon Gordon for convincing my stubborn self that I needed to write stand alone fables, for investing in me, and for never giving up on me even when I frustrate you to no end! I'm very grateful for all your support over the years!

Thank you to all the people who have given me the great privilege and responsibility of mentoring you and speaking into the lives of those you lead. I have learned so much, and I am truly grateful for the opportunity to work with you.

Thank you Jesus for your extravagant, reckless, relentless, and undeserved love.

The Stonecutter's Credo first came into my life on February 7th, 2017, sitting on the steps of the *Embassy Suites* bar in Atlanta, the night before I was giving a talk to *Unified.* The CEO of *Unified*, Steve Powell, shared the story of how Mike Arbour taped the credo to his kids' bathroom mirrors and shares it with colleagues everywhere he went. I assumed there was a book about the stonecutter, and definitely one titled, *pound the stone,* but there wasn't. As soon as I realized this hole existed in the marketplace on February 10th, I made a decision that day that this book would be available for purchase within 3 months. I think I'll end up being off by a few weeks, but we went from idea to full story in less than 2 months, which is a testament to my ghost writer and secret sauce ninja, Jacob Roman. I'm grateful to you Steve for sharing the credo with me!

# Thank YOU to the *Pound The Stone* secret mission group that helped make this story better and helped it launch well!

Tonja Parr. Bengie Parr. Donene Taylor. Joe Alves. Jeff Pellegrini. Greg Towne. Ryan Redondo. Dan Mahany. Bill Phillips. Rosalyn Powell. Sean Armstrong. Heather Dennen. Glenn Monterey. Joseph Raby. Tom Solomon. Tammy Ruehrwein. Cristina Lowery. Aaron Holman. Andrew Greer. Ben White. Daniel Meadows. Rachel Williams. John Torrey. Jeanette Davey. Meg Ortiz. Deb Wagner. Jonathan Heeren. Dustin Krause. Len McKnatt. Natalie Harding. John Leonzo. James Metz. Jennie Warren. Scott Norris. Ashley Wheeler. Meleisa Stockel. Kathy Hughes. Stefani Web. Nic Manogue. Monique Gordon. Raul Garcia. Nate Crandall. Chris Wilbricht. Alexa Kalata. Andria Lamp. Derrick Hastler. Joy Ellefson. Stuart Creamer. Reba Quattlebaum. Nate Sanderson. Timothy Strader. Manny Suarez. Holly Vaught. Donna Bingham. Shane Sowden. Naomi Sugg. Lacie Brown. Steve Thompson. Casey Hill. Kimberly Ganey. Mark Penny. Sarah Condra. Jeff Miller. Jenn Miller. Kay Luedtke. Missy Gerst. Tom Solomon. David Alexander. J.P. Nerbun. Curtis Thompson. Will McCrotty. AnnMarie Ellsworth. Nick Grassi. Noel Emenhiser. Melanie Bradberry. Meagan Price. Paige McVity. Angie Humphries. Brian Knight. Jen Jensen. Carisa Borello. Ben Pellicani. Gloria Papa. Jeff Dahl. Steve Powell. Jill Acosta. Missy Gerst. Pamela Mark. Robbie Sprague. Jeremiah Bartsch. Kelsey Schrimpf. Brock Thompson. Greg Blythe. Brad Conway. Shelly Hotzler.

Made in the USA
Columbia, SC
01 December 2020

25923667R00155